COACHING FOR PEAK EMPLOYEE PERFORMANCE

A Practical Guide To Supporting Employee Development

Bill Foster
Karen R. Seeker

Jossey-Bass
Pfeiffer
San Francisco

RICHARD
CHANG
ASSOCIATES

Printed in the United States of America

Published by

350 Sansome Street, 5th Floor
San Francisco, California 94104-1342
(415) 433-1740; Fax (415) 433-0499
(800) 274-4434; Fax (800) 569-0443

Visit our website at: www.pfeiffer.com

Printing   10   9   8   7   6   5   4   3   2   1

ACKNOWLEDGMENTS

About The Authors

Bill Foster, Managing Director, Publications Division for Richard Chang Associates, Inc., is a practicing manager and trainer with over twelve years of experience in helping others perform better. With a strong background in leadership development, customer service, and selling skills, he has worked with organizations in more than thirty countries.

Karen R. Seeker, a Senior Consultant for Richard Chang Associates, Inc., is highly skilled in the areas of performance improvement, process management, reengineering, and strategic planning. For over twelve years she has led numerous commercial, government, and academic organizations to improve their performance, specializing in high-tech research and development environments, as well as major corporate providers.

The authors would like to acknowledge the support of the entire team of professionals at Richard Chang Associates, Inc. for their contribution to the guidebook development process. In addition, special thanks are extended to the many client organizations who have helped us shape the practical ideas and proven methods shared in this guidebook.

Additional Credits

Editor:	Paul Jerome and Ruth Stingley
Reviewers:	Shirley Codrey, Susan Parker, and Pamela Wade
Graphic Layout:	Christina Slater
Cover Design:	Eric Strand and John Odam Design Associates

PREFACE

The 1990's have already presented individuals and organizations with some very difficult challenges to face and overcome. So who will have the advantage as we move toward the year 2000 and beyond?

The advantage will belong to those with a commitment to continuous learning. Whether on an individual basis or as an entire organization, one key ingredient to building a continuous learning environment is *The Practical Guidebook Collection* brought to you by the Publications Division of Richard Chang Associates, Inc.

After understanding the future *"learning needs"* expressed by our clients and other potential customers, we are pleased to publish *The Practical Guidebook Collection*. These guidebooks are designed to provide you with proven, *"real-world"* tips, tools, and techniques—on a wide range of subjects—that you can apply in the workplace and/or on a personal level immediately.

Once you've had a chance to benefit from *The Practical Guidebook Collection*, please share your feedback with us. We've included a brief *Evaluation and Feedback Form* at the end of the guidebook that you can fax to us at (949) 727-7007.

With your feedback, we can continuously improve the resources we are providing through the Publications Division of Richard Chang Associates, Inc.

Wishing you successful reading,

Richard Y. Chang
President and CEO
Richard Chang Associates, Inc.

TABLE OF CONTENTS

"We cannot direct the wind but we can adjust our sails."

City of Hope

CHAPTER ONE

INTRODUCTION

Most likely, you can recall someone in your life who has coached you. Perhaps it was a sports coach, a dance coach, a speech coach, a teacher, or even one of your parents. This person helped you set goals, tutored you, analyzed your failures, spurred you on to greater achievements, and maybe even motivated you to succeed.

Likewise, you also have stepped into the coaching role at some time or another. It's possible that you've given a stranger directions on the street, provided encouragement to a friend who has had a setback, or coached your child's sports team. You already possess the natural abilities to begin using successful coaching techniques in your work. The key is learning how to more fully develop these abilities.

Coaching is a time-honored way of helping others achieve peak performance. It's no wonder that smart organizations and smart managers are adopting this method for themselves.

Coaching does not come easily to everyone, however. Just because you are a manager doesn't mean you know how to coach. But it is a process that can be learned.

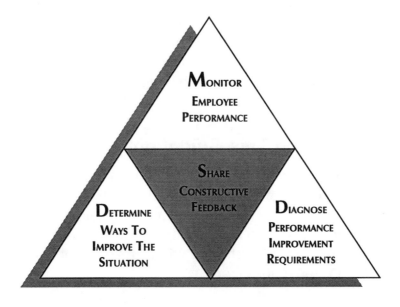

Why Read This Guidebook?

Not only will this guidebook supply you with the tools and techniques for improved performance coaching, it will also show you how to use a four-part Coaching Model to improve employee success. Coaching is central to performance management. And the Coaching Model gives you a process to develop your employees, manage their performance, and hold them accountable for their individual performance plans.

Coaching is not a spectator sport. To coach effectively, you need to actively work with the individuals who report to you. Observation alone is not enough. You need tools to document their progress, determine deficiencies, identify trends, and give feedback. This guidebook gives you the everyday tools needed to effectively build your employees' performance.

All managers want their employees to give their best effort and performance. When individuals succeed in reaching their performance targets, the organization prospers. Coaching plays a key role in that success. This guidebook will help you become a more effective coach.

Who Should Read This Guidebook?

Coaching For Peak Employee Performance will benefit anyone who is responsible for the performance of individuals. It is written for managers, supervisors, team leaders, Human Resources personnel, and trainers. If you want to improve the performance of your staff and have control over the destiny of yourself, your work, and your employees, this guidebook is for you.

This guidebook is also suitable for those of you who work in a service-related industry or a manufacturing environment, whether you work for a profit or a nonprofit organization. Managers in all types of organizations have found coaching to be an effective means of achieving peak performance.

When And How To Use It

Performance management is an ongoing responsibility. The fact is, you probably have employees now whose performance you need to monitor closely, others with whom you need to make adjustments to their plans, and still others whose performance you want to recognize and reinforce. Coaching plays a part in each of these situations. This guidebook will help you become a more effective coach.

Read this guidebook to learn how to:

Coach

♦ Conduct more productive coaching sessions

♦ Structure everyday interactions with team members in ways that build toward success

♦ Diagnose performance problems and provide the right kind of support to every team member

♦ Increase the likelihood of having all employees reach their performance targets

Developing individuals is a strategy that pays off. When individuals succeed, their organization succeeds. Coaching is the process that helps everyone achieve peak performance.

Note: Throughout this guidebook, *"work group"* and *"team"* will be used interchangeably to mean the staff members of your department, division, a special-purpose committee, a task force, etc. The people on your staff are defined as team members, which is also the same as employees, associates, and work group members. Likewise, managers and supervisors sometimes are referred to as team leaders.

THE BIG PICTURE

You're probably eager to begin learning about the four-part Coaching Model you'll use to develop your group of employees into a winning team. Before describing the model, however, you need to have a clear picture of how coaching fits into the Performance Management Cycle.

The Performance Management Cycle

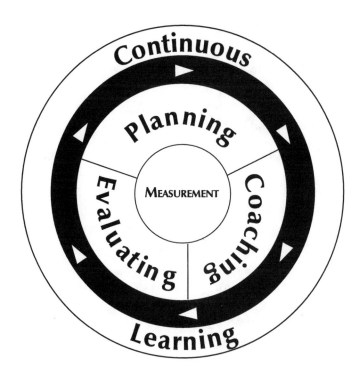

Coaching is only part of the continuous cycle that managers can use to improve individual employee performance on the job. Planning and evaluating also help you boost your team members' performance. The key to both successful coaching and evaluating is a well-designed game plan. It makes sense, then, that the first phase of the Performance Management Cycle is the Planning Phase.

In the Planning Phase of the Performance Management Cycle, the manager *(team leader),* and employee *(team member)* work together to lay the groundwork that establishes the objectives for the employee to be successful. It is in the Planning Phase that the following three components are generated:

---

1. **The Position Description,** which is revised *(or drafted, if it is a new position)* to clearly define general responsibilities and evaluation measurements.

2. **Performance Objectives,** which define specific, individual objectives in the areas of projects, processes, business as usual, and core values for which the employee will be held accountable.

3. **Performance Action Plans,** which define the course of action needed to achieve each objective.

The Planning Phase is the prerequisite to the next phase of the cycle—Coaching. In the Coaching Phase, the finalized and agreed-upon plans are monitored, and you *(as coach)* will provide direction, support, and feedback on an as-needed basis.

In this guidebook, you will learn how to document specific behaviors for each of your team members, diagnose performance improvement requirements *(which may be related to skill, knowledge, motivation, or confidence deficiencies),* determine ways to support your employees, and share constructive feedback.

In the final phase of the Performance Management Cycle—Evaluating—you'll assess each team member's performance. Many organizations refer to such evaluations as *"formal performance appraisals or evaluations."* If you've completed both the Planning and Coaching Phases, evaluating your team members' performance will be much easier.

Performance Management Cycle

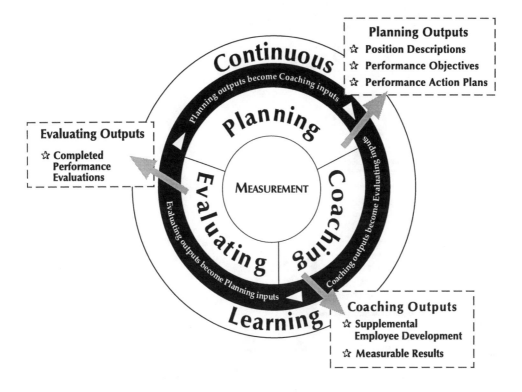

The Performance Management Cycle is an ongoing, continuous operation complete with inputs, processes, and outputs that are interdependent and measurable. The entire cycle is designed to help employees directly contribute to achieving work group and organizational objectives, Key Indicators, and Key Result Areas *(or those areas defined by upper management as critical to the success of the organization)*. The method and process for defining these areas are described in the Measurement Linkage Model. For a complete description of this model, please refer to *Measuring Organizational Improvement Impact* (MOII), published by Richard Chang Associates, Inc.

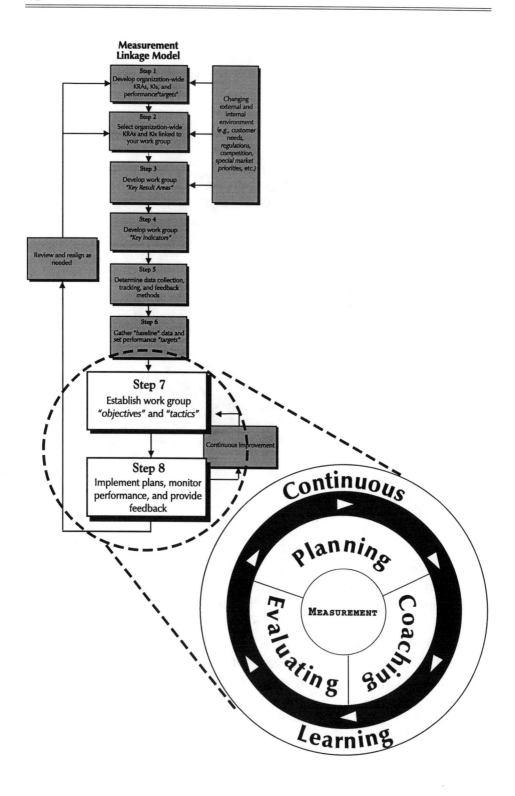

Measurement Linkage Model

Step 1
Develop organization-wide KRAs, KIs, and performance "targets"

Step 2
Select organization-wide KRAs and KIs linked to your work group

Step 3
Develop work group "Key Result Areas"

Step 4
Develop work group "Key Indicators"

Step 5
Determine data collection, tracking, and feedback methods

Step 6
Gather "baseline" data and set performance "targets"

Step 7
Establish work group "objectives" and "tactics"

Step 8
Implement plans, monitor performance, and provide feedback

Changing external and internal environment (e.g., customer needs, regulations, competition, special market priorities, etc.)

Review and realign as needed

Continuous improvement

Continuous

Planning

Coaching

MEASUREMENT

Evaluating

Learning

What Is/Isn't Coaching?

In general, the job of the coach is to help the team win. As coach, your motives, attitude, and actions are all focused on winning.

Coaches are motivators of people and teams. They inspire others to work hard and continually improve. They are the consummate observer and subject-matter expert. They may not be able to play at the same level as their star players, but that's okay. They don't have to. The task of a coach is to help others perform better.

As organizations continue to move toward a team-based environment, the analogy between a sports coach of a team and the organizational coach in the workplace becomes even more similar.

People don't come to work wanting to be poor performers. Given a choice, people prefer to win at work. In fact, most people come to work wanting to be better than average—to excel!

Why not set your team members up for success by coaching them to win? Once you've created and finalized an appropriate performance plan, your day-to-day coaching becomes the most critical contributor to success in performance management.

While a coach can often be a mentor, coaching should not be confused with mentoring. A mentor can be anyone within the organization, or even from outside the organization, and can be either formal or informal. A mentor is a trusted tutor or guide who plays an active role in the development of an individual. And while a coach is not always a mentor, a coach can help identify appropriate mentoring opportunities and facilitate the creation of a mentor/mentee relationship.

Also, a coach is not a counselor. The role of counselor is better suited for professionals such as psychologists, therapists, lawyers, doctors, and the clergy, who are more adept at dealing with counselor-specific needs. Coaching is better suited for the behavioral side of people management. At times, there's a fine line between being a coach and being a counselor. However, it must be made clear that when coaching for performance, a coach is not obligated to *"fix an individual."* Coaches need only focus on monitoring and improving the individual behaviors on the job.

As the coach of your team, you are responsible for the quality of work produced by your direct reports. Do not assume that once they learn a skill they will not need any further coaching. A coach must continually provide varying degrees of direction and support. It's an ongoing process.

Successful work facilitation, like many other management skills, depends upon how well you handle any particular situation, given the task-related skills, knowledge, motivation, and confidence of the team member. In order to facilitate the work of others, a coach must:

- ◆ Ensure proper training of team members
- ◆ Provide necessary resources
- ◆ Look for ways to help
- ◆ Know the personal preferences of all members
- ◆ Share information
- ◆ Give constructive feedback
- ◆ Facilitate problem solving
- ◆ Provide appropriate amount of direction and/or support

Why Coach?

There is a strong need for managers to become great coaches. If you doubt this, ask yourself the following question:

> *"How much of the knowledge you possess and currently use on the job did you learn in school?"*

The typical response will be *"not a lot."* Even if you ask a technical person who puts his technical training to use every day, you'll still find that the invaluable tips, tricks, and shortcuts that make the job easier were picked up informally on the job. And, with the amount of change occurring in organizations today, continuous learning is now a way of life.

Ongoing coaching is a way to support ongoing learning and development. By avoiding outside training sessions that eat up time as well as money, coaches can directly impart valuable information to team members. Team members can immediately put these new skills to use and practice them under the supervision of the coach. If outside training is still needed, the coach will determine the type of training needed, whether it is a five-day, intensive workshop, or simply the observation of another team member performing the task.

Winning organizations will also maximize their training investment when coaching is used to reinforce outside training. Immediate support both before and after outside training sessions will ensure that new skills are put to use before the impact of the training session wears off.

Performance Objectives

Coaching

Organizations that have made coaching an everyday part of employee development have realized many benefits. Some of them include:

♦ **More exceptional employees**
Wouldn't you prefer to hire a few outstanding people to get the job done? Coaching helps individuals grow and develop new skills that will make them more valuable to your organization. Typically, you coach people until they become self-starters and solve their own problems. In turn, someday these people may become excellent coaches.

♦ **Reduced turnover**
Individuals want to excel at what they do. It feels good. When employees are rewarded at work with new challenges and growth, they are less likely to become dissatisfied. This saves the organization the overwhelming costs of hiring new people and bolsters organizational morale.

♦ **Improved interpersonal relationships**
Frequent check-ins with the team members you are coaching will result in increased communication and fewer misunderstandings. Even if the time you spend together is limited, key issues will be discussed and clarified. Effective coaches use this time together to recognize and reward good behaviors.

Do you really have a choice not to coach? With organizations becoming flatter, and managers gaining more and more direct reports, it's challenging to help everyone achieve their objectives. As a result, the amount of time a coach can spend with each team member is limited.

Therefore, these short time allotments are critical turning points in the performance of the team members. In many organizations, managers are feeling stretched and pulled from all sides.

Wouldn't it be nice if:

♦ All team members knew what they will be held accountable for this year *(as determined in the Planning Phase)?*

♦ And that when you got to performance evaluations *(in the Evaluating Phase),* you had clear, concise files on your team members, which described their progress over the course of the year with respect to their performance plans?

The tools in this guidebook, which you will use during the Coaching Phase, will not only bring order to any chaos, but will provide you with the information you need to appropriately evaluate employee performance. Now, doesn't that sound like a worthwhile game plan?

Understanding The Coaching Model

You now understand that coaching is critical to improving employee performance. And, you understand what is meant by coaching, and when it may be most needed. Now it is time to learn a four-part model that is central to the responsibilities of day-to-day coaching.

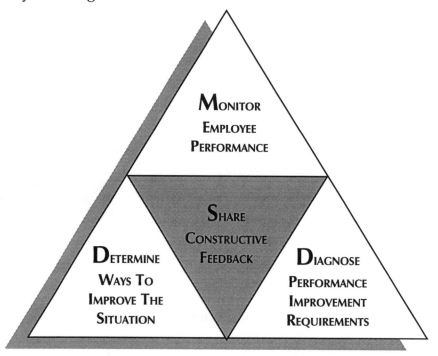

Each part or component of the Coaching Model is central to the task of people management. These parts are not linear steps. Each part is dependent upon the development needs of your employees. For some team members, you will need to utilize all four components on a regular basis in order to stay on track. Eventually, you'll find your peak performers implementing these elements for themselves. Your goal as coach is to develop your employees to the point where they monitor their own work, diagnose their own performance improvement requirements, and determine ways to improve the situation. However, you should continue to monitor performance and provide feedback on an ongoing basis for everyone on your team.

Monitor employee performance

In this first component of the Coaching Model, you will use the outputs of the Planning Phase *(i.e., Position Description, Performance Objectives, and Performance Action Plans)* to indicate the roles, responsibilities, actions, and measurements that you and each of your team members have agreed will form the basis for this year's workload. You will observe each team member's performance in these areas, and document behaviors indicating success or failure in carrying out these duties.

Diagnose performance improvement requirements

As the behaviors are monitored, you will need to determine if the behaviors you observe are appropriate to meet the performance objectives. You will determine if each behavior either meets, exceeds, or does not meet expectations. If the behaviors do not meet expectations *(and are therefore deficient)*, this indicates a type of problem. Deficiencies can be one of at least four types: *knowledge, skill, motivation,* or *confidence.* You must determine which type of deficiency this team member is demonstrating and translate it into a performance improvement requirement.

Determine ways to improve the situation

Once a performance improvement requirement is identified, you will determine the appropriate type of direction and/or support, and the extent to which it is needed. Direction involves telling or showing your team member(s) what to do, how to do it, when to do it, and where to do it. Support also comes in many varieties, including training, listening, problem solving, peer mentoring, demonstrations, practice time, readings, and so on. You will then work with the team member to get him what he needs, when he needs it.

Share constructive feedback

Sharing feedback is ongoing and continual; therefore, it should be developed and delivered in a constructive, caring way. However, ultimately it is important to determine if the direction and/or support you provided helped or not. If it did, celebrate together. If it didn't, provide constructive feedback and then return to the first component of the Coaching Model (*Monitor Employee Performance*) to observe new behaviors, diagnose requirements, determine new ways to support, and try again.

In the next four chapters, you will learn more about each of these four components. Each part of the Coaching Model is designed to help you help your people achieve peak performance. And don't forget that measurement also plays an important role in coaching.

The Need For Measurement

> *If you can't measure it, you can't manage it.*

In the Planning Phase you established measurable objectives for your team members to accomplish. During the Coaching Phase, ongoing measurement is a critical component to both individual and organizational success.

Imagine going through school and not getting back any tests, essays, quizzes, or papers of any kind all year. Then, at the end of the year, you get one aggregate mark. You wouldn't know whether you did well in math or science. You wouldn't know how your efforts to study for different tests paid off. You wouldn't know what you did right or wrong so that you could learn from it and improve the next time. That one grade at the end of the year would be meaningless.

Measurement is essential to coaching. The more accurate the measurement, the better you can manage. It's these measurements that are critical to the organization's success—and yours. Too often, productivity, budget compliance, and other cost-related measures are overemphasized. While cost-reduction measures are critical, they should be balanced with measures of service, quality, leadership, employee flexibility, and continuous improvement.

As you observe and monitor performance, diagnose performance requirements, determine ways to improve the situation, and provide constructive feedback, be certain to include measurements as an ongoing, continuous coaching behavior. It's your duty and responsibility. And, it will make your job a lot easier, too.

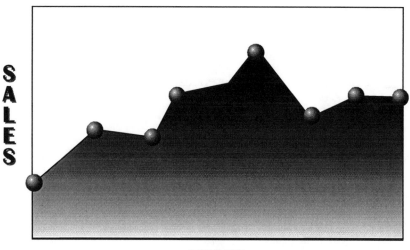

TIME

CHAPTER TWO WORKSHEET: SHOULD YOU TACKLE COACHING IN YOUR ORGANIZATION?

1. Which of the following characteristics of an effective coach does your organization encourage you to develop? Check all that apply.

_____ Ensures proper training.

_____ Furnishes necessary resources.

_____ Looks for ways to help.

_____ Knows personal preferences.

_____ Shares information.

_____ Provides constructive feedback.

_____ Facilitates problem solving.

_____ Provides appropriate amount of direction and/or support.

2. Describe the role a coach plays in your organization.

_____

_____

_____

_____

_____

_____

3. Effective coaching results in benefits to both you and your organization. Write down the benefits you hope to gain through coaching.

_____

_____

_____

_____

_____

_____

_____

MONITOR EMPLOYEE PERFORMANCE

Successful coaching requires good observation methods. Unless you know how your team members are performing, you can't help them achieve their potential. In this chapter, you'll be given the methods for documenting, tracking, and monitoring employee performance throughout the year.

Why Document?

Have you ever assessed an individual's performance during the annual performance evaluation based solely on your memory? It doesn't work very well, does it? Unless you have a photographic memory that holds fast to every detail, you can't rely on your memory to adequately evaluate performance.

Johnston, an environmental-design supervisor,...

sat down to fill out the performance evaluation sheets for each of the nine team members reporting to him. *"In my opinion,"* Johnston muttered to himself, *"this is the worst part of my job as supervisor. Oh well,"* he sighed, *"I have to start somewhere. Maybe I'll start with Andrea. I think she did pretty well this year. I didn't get any complaints from the customers she supports, and she wasn't in my office much. Wait a second! Wasn't it Andrea who created the conflict with purchasing that created my biggest nightmare? No, I think it was Tran. No, I remember now. It was Alexi."* Johnston hit the top of his desk with his fist. *"I can't even remember who was responsible for that fiasco!"...*

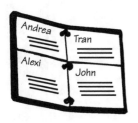

If Johnston had created document files on each of his team members, he wouldn't have found himself in such a dilemma. One of the primary goals of coaching is to provide the information and input for the Evaluating Phase. An easy, painless way to obtain this information is through the use of document files.

The benefits of document files are numerous. Document files provide:

◆ A detailed record of employee performance

By recording information throughout the year, you can see the progress each individual employee is making toward achieving organizational and personal objectives. You have a vehicle for discussing employee performance, and recorded evidence to support these discussions.

◆ A reference for future decisions

Perhaps you have a new task that needs to be completed or a new position that has just opened, and you're confident one of your team members would be perfect for it. Your document files contain information about the specific behaviors each individual has demonstrated. You can check to see if this team member has exhibited the behaviors that would suggest she would be successful at the new task or in the new position.

◆ A record to guard against legal actions

Even though you might not like to admit it, some employee disputes, layoffs, or firings result in legal disputes. Differences can be resolved more easily in court *(or in arbitration)* if files and records exist. These files become your justification in legal situations. Make sure that all documents which contain sensitive information related to potential separation are kept with your Human Resources department.

◆ An opportunity for managers to get involved

Oftentimes, managers and supervisors get caught up in their own tasks, and lose sight of what their team members are actually doing on a regular basis. Document files reinforce actions which keep them in direct touch with each employee.

Laura, a customer-service manager...

for a major retailer, was facing a lawsuit. One of her employees, Don, was frequently late, which affected everyone in the department. Laura had told him that if he continued to come in late, it could result in him being terminated. Although she warned him of the consequences of his behavior, she did not document his behavior nor her warnings. When he finally got fired, Don claimed *"unfair treatment"* and decided to sue....

Unfortunately, many supervisors don't document employee performance on an ongoing basis. Why?

"I don't know what to write!"

"I'm sure I'll remember their behavior."

"I'm already overloaded!"

"I don't have time!"

"I'm just not organized!"

"I keep forgetting!"

If you don't document now, you can expect that sooner or later you'll have to invest significant time to recreate situations, whether for performance evaluations, for making informed decisions, or even in front of a lawyer to back up your allegations. Documentation is critical to your success as a coach.

Establishing The Documentation

You should already have a file on each employee that contains the outputs of the Planning Phase. In other words, you should have in your possession a copy of your employees' performance plans. For a complete description of this phase, please refer to *Planning Successful Employee Performance*, published by Richard Chang Associates, Inc. It is your employee's progress toward their plans that you will monitor, document, and support throughout the Coaching Phase of the Performance Management Cycle.

In addition to the performance plans, you will establish a file for each team member that includes:

Performance Plans
Position Description
Performance Progress Sheet(s)

The Performance Progress Sheet

The Performance Progress Sheet is designed to help you:

1. Track observable behaviors throughout the year that indicate progress *(or lack thereof)* toward performance objectives *(which were defined during the Planning Phase)*

2. Assess team members' behavior in the most appropriate category*(ies)*—knowledge, skill, motivation, or confidence

3. Document winning performance as a strength and an opportunity for positive feedback

4. Work together with your team members to define their actual performance problem(s) and their requirements

5. Determine together *(or research separately)* the type of support *(solution)* that will enable your employees to achieve their objectives

6. Track both the target and completion dates for getting the needed support

An example of this form can be found in the Appendix. You may want to reproduce and use it, or you may have a different format which works better for you. In either case, in the monitoring part of the Coaching Model you will fill in only a portion of the Performance Progress Sheet. The form itself includes:

◆ The employee's name, coach's name, and period of performance

◆ The date of the observed behavior

◆ The specific observed behavior that you are monitoring

◆ A diagnosis as to the cause of the behavior

◆ An action plan to improve or capitalize on the situation

◆ Results of the action plan upon a revisit of the situation

The reason why this part of the Coaching Model is called *"monitoring"* is because no subjectivity belongs here. You are not to add your opinions. You should only be concerned with the actual tracking of what you or someone else observed the team member doing on the job. This becomes the data you collect.

Monitoring Observable Behaviors

When monitoring, you must concern yourself with specific, observable behaviors. Don't include assumptions or rumors. Define your team members' performance in terms of what they are doing right now. Don't express the behavior in terms of what they can't do, but what they are doing.

Consider the following example:

Misha has a performance objective...

to *"develop a plan for increasing distribution channels for birthday wrapping paper by 20 percent by July 1, XXXX."* Misha's supervisor, Taylor, has prepared a Performance Progress Sheet for her. Taylor is now prepared to list Misha's behaviors as he observes them.

During a staff meeting in late January, Misha did not have much to report on her plan. Taylor documented this behavior back at the office, and dated it 1/22/XX. He thought that he would allow more time before assuming Misha needed support. The next day he strolled by and asked how things were going, and observed Misha having difficulty writing objectives for the plan. After answering some of Misha's questions, he documented this behavior as well *(which can be found on pages 28 and 29).*

It is important not to overreact at each and every potential problem. It is also important to distinguish between actual behaviors and assumptions. For example, if Harry, a pharmaceutical sales representative reporting to you, continues to turn in incomplete sales reports, you would document *"Incomplete sales report on X date."* on Harry's Performance Progress Sheet.

However, do not assume that Harry either is too lazy to complete his sales reports, doesn't know how to fill them out, or doesn't have time to finish. While it's possible that one of these three examples is the reason for his incomplete reports, you won't know for sure until you investigate further.

Collecting Performance Data

Collecting performance data does not involve scientific methodology or sneak attacks. In fact, it's quite simple. Following are three suggested methods for collecting performance data.

1. Observations

Directly observe behavior. Sounds easy enough, doesn't it? Observations do not need to be done secretly; instead, you can ask your team members to demonstrate parts of their job for you. It is important that you be authentic, not sneaky.

In addition, it is important that you assure your team members that your observations are for developmental purposes, not evaluation. Look closely for tasks that they do well *(or ones that they don't do well)*. Know what you are looking for ahead of time, and take time to think through what it takes to perform well in the area you are observing.

In the case of a team member working on a new objective, you may not see expected behavior the first time. This is normal. In response, you will want to acknowledge progress toward *"almost right"* behavior and provide additional direction.

PERFORMANCE

Employee Misha	Position/Title Account Representative	Coach Taylor

DATE	BEHAVIOR	DIAGNOSIS
	Describe the behavior observed using specific examples and the impacts of the behavior.	Diagnose the cause of the behavior (*i.e., knowledge, skill, motivation, confidence deficiency*). Or, if strength, list the reason.
1/22	Provided incomplete information on the new plan for increasing distribution channels. Missing information prevents the completion of overall department plan.	
1/23	After asking Misha for the report, she was still unable to complete the new plan. This caused further delay of the department plan.	

PROGRESS SHEET

Department National Sales	Period of Performance 1/1/XX — 12/31/XX
ACTION PLAN	**RESULTS**
Create an action plan to improve the situation or capitalize on the strength. Decide on specific measurements and evaluation methods along with target date(s).	Revisit the situation and determine if the behavior meets the desired results.

2. Input from others

In some cases, you will need to solicit help from other parties who may have had the opportunity to observe the individual's behavior.

Others you could ask include:

- ◆ peers
- ◆ other managers
- ◆ other departments (particularly internal customers and suppliers)
- ◆ external customers
- ◆ external suppliers

Again, you'll need to know what you are asking for ahead of time. Be specific and direct, and ask others what they have directly observed. Steer away from opinions of the team members—focus on objective observations.

3. Status meetings *(both formal and informal)*

Ask the team member himself! He knows better than anyone else whether things are tough or easy. While your team members should be the first to ask for help, they may not unless you let them know that it's okay to do so. If you endorse queries for help, you'll spend less time investigating in your job as coach.

To get the most out of monitoring, ask yourself the following questions:

♦ Does the team member's performance meet organizational standards?

♦ Are there complaints from the employee's peers?

♦ Does the team member demonstrate enthusiasm and initiative for her work?

♦ How well are customers satisfied with what they receive from the employee?

♦ How does the team member's performance compare with others in similar positions?

♦ How well does the individual multi-task?

♦ How well does the employee handle suggestions or direction from you?

♦ To what extent does the team member seem stressed?

♦ To what extent is the employee's workspace useable?

Above all else, remember that the purpose of the data collected here is not to evaluate, intimidate, or otherwise make your team member feel uncomfortable. The purpose of monitoring and documenting performance is to form the basis for providing appropriate support.

Your goal is peak performance. You want each team member to become more successful, which makes you more successful; and, in turn, makes your organization more successful. It's a win-win situation for all involved. Or, better yet, it could be called an all-win situation!

CHAPTER THREE WORKSHEET: KEEPING TRACK OF YOUR TEAM MEMBERS' PERFORMANCE

1. How often do you currently observe your employees' behavior?

_____

_____

_____

_____

_____

2. Do you keep document files (*i.e., Performance Progress Sheets, incident files, praising letters*)? If yes, describe what you keep in each of the files.

_____

_____

_____

_____

_____

_____

_____

3. Think of one of your team members and a current behavior you observed that team member exhibit. Then use the Performance Progress Sheet on the next page and fill out the following information for your team member:

- ♦ The team member's name, position/title, coach, department, and period of performance

- ♦ The date of the observed behavior

- ♦ The actual, specific observed behavior and the impact of that behavior

PERFORMANCE

Employee	Position/Title	Coach

DATE	BEHAVIOR	DIAGNOSIS
	Describe the behavior observed using specific examples and the impacts of the behavior.	Diagnose the cause of the behavior (*i.e., knowledge, skill, motivation, confidence deficiency*). Or, if strength, list the reason.

PROGRESS SHEET

Department	Period of Performance
ACTION PLAN	**RESULTS**
Create an action plan to improve the situation or capitalize on the strength. Decide on specific measurements and evaluation methods along with target date(s).	Revisit the situation and determine if the behavior meets the desired results.

DIAGNOSE PERFORMANCE IMPROVEMENT REQUIREMENTS

Monitoring your team members' performance is usually the first step in your job as coach. And, it's definitely an important step. You need to observe behaviors before you can diagnose your employees' performance improvement requirements. Think of it in medical terms. Every doctor needs to know a patient's symptoms before she can diagnose an illness.

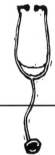

If you've done your documentation work, you will have documented several specific behaviors for your team members. Those specific behaviors should indicate performance toward their individual objectives. The next questions to ask yourself are:

> Do the behaviors I've listed suggest that this team member can accomplish the performance objective?
>
> Or, do the behaviors listed suggest that this person needs direction or support from me, the coach?

How you answer determines what you will do next.

Recognizing Behaviors As Deficiencies

If you wish to be an effective coach, you must develop the ability to determine if your employees are demonstrating the capability of achieving their objectives and carrying out their responsibilities. You have to be both observant and insightful. If your team members are struggling, you must be able to provide the appropriate level and type of support they need. Remember, this is the primary function of the coach—to help your team win. You're only as strong as your weakest link.

Before you can offer the appropriate direction or support, you must first understand and diagnose the type of problem each employee is facing. If a team member is not performing as well as needed, any number of reasons may be responsible. For instance, the team member may not:

- ◆ Understand how to find the information he needs

- ◆ Have the competence to complete the task

- ◆ Have access to a complete set of directions

- ◆ Want to do the assignment in the way it was designed

- ◆ Believe the task is valued in the organization

- ◆ Have the ability to complete the assignment

In each of these situations, the reason for the employee not performing differs. Reasons for (*or causes of*) poor performance are sometimes referred to as *"deficiencies."* Deficiencies usually tend to fall into one or more of four categories:

- ◆ Lack of knowledge
- ◆ Lack of skill
- ◆ Lack of motivation
- ◆ Lack of confidence

In addition, your employees may be restricted by other types of deficiencies which contribute to poor performance, but which cannot be resolved through coaching. Examples include:

- ◆ Lack of technology
- ◆ Lack of policies/procedures
- ◆ Lack of vision/strategic intent of the organization
- ◆ Lack of tools

In these instances, you can request additional resources or recommend that upper management provide more guidance. However, in the categories of knowledge, skills, motivation, and confidence, it's up to you to provide specific coaching expertise that will help your team members reach peak performance. It is your job as coach to determine which category best applies and to what extent the employee is demonstrating deficient *(or outstanding)* behaviors related to the category.

A correct diagnosis is critical. For example, say that you have scheduled one team member to mentor another because you believe that person doesn't understand how to use the computer software. In reality, however, the team member is not producing the document needed because she is being asked by your boss to produce viewgraphs for his speech instead. In this case, your diagnosis is incorrect, and the mentoring time you've scheduled could very well be a waste of time.

Take a look at the following Performance Progress Sheet that was introduced in the previous chapter. If you have completed the monitoring step, you should have documented one or several behaviors by now.

PERFORMANCE

Employee	Position/Title	Coach
Misha	Account Representative	Taylor

	BEHAVIOR	DIAGNOSIS
DATE	Describe the behavior observed using specific examples and the impacts of the behavior.	Diagnose the cause of the behavior (*i.e., knowledge, skill, motivation, confidence deficiency*). Or, if strength, list the reason.
1/22	Provided incomplete information on the new plan for increasing distribution channels. Missing information prevents the completion of overall department plan.	
1/23	After asking Misha for the report, she was still unable to complete the new plan. This caused further delay of the department plan.	
2/10	Sales performance for January was 115% to goal. Revenue and profits were above projections which helps organizational growth.	

PROGRESS SHEET

ACTION PLAN	RESULTS
Department National Sales	**Period of Performance** 1/1/XX — 12/31/XX
ACTION PLAN	**RESULTS**
Create an action plan to improve the situation or capitalize on the strength. Decide on specific measurements and evaluation methods along with target date(s).	Revisit the situation and determine if the behavior meets the desired results.

Your next activity is to determine what the behavior you have documented suggests. Specifically, ask yourself the following questions:

- ◆ Does the behavior indicate a weakness or a strength?

- ◆ Does the behavior tend to suggest a weakness or strength in one or more of the following four categories?

  - Knowledge
  - Skill
  - Motivation
  - Confidence

- ◆ Where does the behavior fall within the selected category?

  - Exceeds expectations
  - Meets expectations
  - Does not meet expectations

Each type of deficiency has reasons *(or causes)* as to why it exists. You must first understand what causes the deficiency so you can then provide the *"correct"* direction and/or support.

A supervisor, Nick,...

thinks one of his team members, Cayla, an order-entry clerk, has an attitude problem. *"No matter how many times I tell Cayla to get me a completed form within twenty minutes of when an order has been placed,"* Nick explained to a colleague, *"she never does. I think she doesn't think it's important. Her attitude needs to change."*

In reality, it's not that Cayla views completing the form as a low-priority task *(which reflects a motivation deficiency)*. Cayla doesn't know the products well enough. Every time an order is placed, she has to go into the warehouse to get information off the product to complete the forms, which adds to the time it takes to complete them. She has a knowledge deficiency, not a motivation deficiency....

Once you have determined that your employee is demonstrating a deficiency, you will need to determine the appropriate category in which it falls.

Determining The Appropriate Category

Have you documented behavior that indicates a deficiency in knowledge, skill, motivation, or confidence? Perhaps it's a combination of one or more of these, or it could be due to a lack of appropriate tools, technology, vision, or policy. How do you know what is responsible for the deficiency?

First of all, don't assume that the answer will be obvious. In many cases, it is best to sit down with the employee and discuss the behavior, and determine together which is the most appropriate category.

At this point, consider a one-on-one meeting with the team member. Use the Performance Progress Sheet as a tool to drive the discussion. Describe in clear, objective terms the behaviors you have noted *(during monitoring)*, and state in which category you believe the behavior falls. Then ask the team member:

◆ Why do you think you are having trouble?

◆ What are some of the factors contributing to the behavior?

◆ Are there other things that might be getting in your way?

◆ How do you feel about falling short of this objective?

Understanding the different categories will help guide the discussion in the appropriate direction. Read through the following descriptions of the different categories. You need to know them before you can attempt to diagnose performance requirements.

Lack of knowledge

Knowledge refers to concepts, principles, procedures, policies, or any other information that your team member might need. It also includes the ability to comprehend and apply that information to implement the job responsibilities.

A lack of knowledge means that the employee doesn't know the needed information to do the job, or doesn't know how to carry out the responsibilities. Neither threats nor rewards will make a difference. If your team member's deficiency is due to a lack of knowledge, he simply doesn't know how to fulfill the job requirements, and therefore, cannot.

Clues which indicate a knowledge deficiency include:

- ◆ An abundance of questions
- ◆ Puzzled looks or expressions
- ◆ Spending excessive time researching
- ◆ Requesting to partner with another team member who is viewed as an expert in this area

Lack of skill

The skill category usually refers to the physical ability needed to accomplish or carry out a task or assignment. Even though a person may intellectually understand how to do a job, she might not possess the skills to do it. One of your team members, for example, might understand the inside and outside of a computer (*e.g., amount of RAM, size of hard drive, interfacing capability, program commands, etc.*), but can't operate it.

The skill category can also refer to technique. For example, the ability to facilitate a group discussion to consensus requires not only the knowledge of good facilitation practices, but also the techniques of managing and directing a group. Techniques such as these must be physically practiced to achieve excellence and, therefore, usually fall into this category.

Clues which indicate a skill deficiency include:

- ◆ Visible misuse of tools or equipment
- ◆ Inability to use a specific technique
- ◆ Not using a new tool immediately
- ◆ Not taking advantage of certain features of tools
- ◆ Avoiding assignments which require usage of tools and/or techniques

Lack of motivation

Attitudes and values are many times lumped together in a category called *"motivation."* It is true that incentives and consequences tend to motivate, and that motivational factors will contribute to employee attitude. Motivation is defined as a person's interest in, and enthusiasm for, the job.

But attitude isn't the only contributor to a lack of motivation. And what is motivational to one person may not be motivational to another. Motivational issues can surface in numerous ways for numerous reasons.

Examples of why an employee may not want to complete a task include:

- ◆ The team member doesn't believe she will be viewed as a valuable asset within the organization

- ◆ The employee's religion does not allow him to work during certain hours

- ◆ The team member feels like he has been manipulated by upper management in taking the assignment

- ◆ The employee disagrees with the approach she is being asked to use

- ◆ The team member won't personally treat any human being in that manner, even if his manager is insisting

- ◆ The employee is being forced to work with another team member with whom she just doesn't get along

- ◆ The team member just doesn't find the work interesting

The types of behavior that fall into this category are those that result because the employee fundamentally disagrees with the assignment in some way. Such behaviors can be difficult to diagnose because they typically require asking a team member to honestly and authentically state why he disagrees with a management request or assignment. This type of self-disclosure is not always comfortable.

On the other hand, some managers tend to jump to the conclusion that an employee has an *"attitude problem"* whenever an assignment is not completed. Often, that is not the case at all.

With organizations becoming more and more diverse, behaviors which fall into this category become more and more important to recognize. Good coaches flex their styles to accommodate differences, and take the time to adjust assignments accordingly.

Clues which indicate a motivation deficiency include:

- Constantly challenging the assignment
- Demonstrated emotions (tears)
- Disagreements and refusal to do the work
- Comparing the assignment to others' work in the organization
- Continually complaining to other team members
- General lack of enthusiasm or interest for the task

Lack of confidence

Behaviors in this category are those associated with a fear of failure. Your team member's self-confidence, notion of self-worth, and secure feelings are overtaken by the fear of failure. An individual may have all the knowledge, skills, and even a really positive attitude, but simply cannot make the plunge to take on a particular assignment.

A lack of confidence appears often when a task requires an individual to give presentations. In fact, the fear of presenting is ranked at the top in several well-known lists of greatest fears.

But confidence is needed to carry out any type of job, whether it is a receptionist feeling confident enough to handle all incoming calls, or an astronaut who needs confidence that the landing gear will engage on the space shuttle.

A lack of confidence is a deficiency which can also be directly related to the work environment. Even if your team member enters a job with confidence and self-esteem, that confidence can be eroded or altered in an environment where:

◆ Fellow workers are not open, honest, or authentic with each other, especially management with staff

◆ The team member has suffered several repeated small failures

◆ There exists the constant need to prove oneself before the organization respects one's abilities

◆ Team interactions demonstrate a lack of trust or a lack of empowerment

Clues which indicate a confidence deficiency include:

◆ Showing resistance to change or completing the task

◆ Lack of interaction with others

◆ Lack of volunteering for new assignments

◆ Praising others, but discounting oneself

◆ Preferring roles which are supportive rather than leading

◆ Completing numerous inconsequential assignments to "look busy" while avoiding the more important and riskier tasks

Documenting The Behavior

Since behaviors tend to vary over time, tracking their progress on an ongoing basis can be helpful. In some cases, you will be tracking progress toward outcomes as opposed to observed behavior such as units produced, sales made, number of orders processed, and so on. Also, be aware that your team members will be more competent on some tasks than they are on others. As such, you will monitor certain tasks more closely than you will others based on the demonstrated skill level of the employee in relation to the task at hand. The Performance Progress Sheet can be a useful form in tracking the progress of behaviors and performance.

The Performance Progress Sheet not only reflects progress, but it also provides a useful instrument for discussion. Even if you and your team member both agree that there is a deficiency, you may disagree on how big the gap really is. One way to track performance level is to rate behaviors according to expectations. That is, does a particular behavior meet expectations, exceed expectations, or fall short of expectations?

When describing team members' behavior in writing, ensure there is little doubt in your communication. Use two to three sentences to describe the behavior or skill in succinct terms, specifically explain how and why the skill contributes to performance, and cite at least one example of a situation where you observed this skill as a strength or an area of needed improvement. The goal is to focus feedback on actual behaviors.

Once documented, you and your team member can determine if the performance objectives are still valid and if there is a need for a change in the type of direction or support from you. This document becomes both an action plan between you and your employee and becomes an excellent source of input for the Evaluation Phase of the Performance Management Cycle. Performance evaluation is covered in detail in the practical guidebook, *Evaluating Employee Performance*, published by Richard Chang Associates, Inc.

PERFORMANCE

Employee Misha	Position/Title Account Representative	Coach Taylor

	BEHAVIOR	DIAGNOSIS
DATE	Describe the behavior observed using specific examples and the impacts of the behavior.	Diagnose the cause of the behavior (*i.e., knowledge, skill, motivation, confidence deficiency*). Or, if strength, list the reason.
1/22	Provided incomplete information on the new plan for increasing distribution channels. Missing information prevents the completion of overall department plan.	May lack confidence in selling to new clients. Prefers to call on existing clients. Chose not to complete plan.
1/23	After asking Misha for the report, she was still unable to complete the new plan. This caused further delay of the department plan.	After further evaluation, it is evident that Misha has a lack of confidence for producing the report.
2/10	Sales performance for January was 115% to goal. Revenue and profits were above projections which helps organizational growth.	Increased skills were a result of increased focus on key accounts and capitalizing on special promotions.

PROGRESS SHEET

Department	Period of Performance
National Sales	1/1/XX — 12/31/XX
ACTION PLAN	**RESULTS**
Create an action plan to improve the situation or capitalize on the strength. Decide on specific measurements and evaluation methods along with target date(s).	Revisit the situation and determine if the behavior meets the desired results.

Why include initials?

There are times when management decisions regarding an employee's progress in an organization are challenged. The document files provide a detailed account of what you have observed, but you must also have a means of verifying that you have shared the information with the team member.

If you don't communicate your documentation with each employee, the team member could suggest unfair treatment, and claim that he didn't know that he wasn't doing well. However, with his initials next to the unacceptable behaviors which required corrective discipline, you will have the proof you need to support any appropriate management decision.

You may be asked to provide proof of discussions in different situations, such as:

♦ Performance reviews

♦ Management meetings

♦ Demotions or transfers

♦ Arbitrations

♦ Terminations or layoffs

♦ Courts of law

In any case, you only protect yourself from unwanted controversy if you find a way to document completely, and indicate that both parties understand the content of the documentation. If you choose a different format, make sure you have a way to get your team member to acknowledge the discussions.

Defining Performance Improvement Requirements

A performance improvement requirement is the gap between current performance and desired performance. Once you understand the deficiency *(or problem)*, you must translate it into a requirement statement. It's this step that is oftentimes overlooked.

Even if you know the category of the deficiency, you may still come up with the wrong solution if you don't fully understand the need. Remember Nick, the supervisor, who believes Cayla, the order-entry clerk, has an attitude problem because she won't fill out the order form as quickly as Nick would like? Read how Nick tries to account for Cayla's deficiency.

In a one-on-one meeting with Cayla,...

Nick learns that Cayla doesn't have an attitude problem, but a knowledge deficiency. Cayla doesn't know the products well enough, so she has to go to the warehouse to fill out her forms. *"I'm going to send you to training,"* Nick told Cayla. *"There you'll learn about the products."* Nick thinks he is being a good coach.

However, Cayla comes back from training even more confused than ever. There are virtually thousands of products she is expected to remember as a result of a two-day workshop. Her feeling of incompetence is increased, her confidence goes down, and her performance declines.

Even though Cayla and Nick were on target about her knowledge deficiency, training was not the appropriate solution. There are too many products for Cayla to remember. A better solution would have been to provide her with a reference or some type of source material which summarizes all the product information to keep at her desk. If Nick would have defined the requirement statement first, it would have clearly suggested a solution. In this case, the statement could read:

> *"Cayla needs to have access to summarized product information quickly."*

Both Nick and Cayla would have realized that training would not have solved this performance improvement requirement.

To further demonstrate how to work your way from documenting observed behaviors to defining a deficiency category and finally to creating a requirement statement, look at the following examples:

Example #1

Observed behavior:
Betty did not meet the scheduled milestone to have the proposal to her manager for review.

Deficiency category:
Betty does not have the required knowledge to draft a training proposal.

Performance improvement requirement:
Betty needs to develop her understanding of the following:

♦ How to define statements of learning objectives

♦ How to use information from similar proposals

♦ How to estimate a project of this nature

Example #2

Observed behavior:
Bob has rescheduled his presentation to the sales department six times.

Deficiency category:
Bob does not have the confidence in his ability to present well.

Performance improvement requirement:
Bob needs to develop the self-esteem and self-assurance required to make comprehensible and fluent presentations. He needs to understand that no presentation is expected to be completely flawless, and that he doesn't have to be positioned as the expert in this area, and that it is okay to say, *"I don't know the answer to that"* if he is confronted with a difficult question.

Once you are able to make the leap from observed behavior to deficiency category to performance improvement requirement, your next step is to determine the appropriate support or direction you should provide to the team member. If you've done your work up to this point, you can be confident that you're traveling in the right direction. You're on your way to leading your team members down the path to performance success.

CHAPTER FOUR WORKSHEET: DIAGNOSING PERFORMANCE IMPROVEMENT REQUIREMENTS

1. Think about the performance of one of your team members who is experiencing difficulty in some area. You may choose the employee you wrote about in the Chapter Three Worksheet *(Question # 3). (If you can't come up with a real-life example, create a hypothetical one.)* To diagnose the performance improvement requirements of your team member, you'll have to determine the category into which the deficiency falls. Check all clues within the categories below that apply to your situation.

Lack Of Knowledge

_____An abundance of questions

_____Puzzled looks or expressions

_____Spending excessive time researching

_____Requesting to partner with another team member who is viewed as an expert in this area

_____Other *(specify)* _____

Lack Of Skill

_____Visible misuse of tools or equipment

_____Inability to use a specific technique

_____Not using a new tool immediately

_____Not taking advantage of certain features of tools

_____ Avoiding assignments which require usage of tools and or/techniques

_____Other *(specify)* _____

Lack Of Motivation

_____Constantly challenging the assignment

_____Demonstrated emotions *(tears)*

_____Disagreements and refusal to do the work

_____Comparing the assignment to others' work in the organization

_____Continually complaining to other team members

_____General lack of enthusiasm or interest for the task

_____Other *(specify)* _____

Lack Of Confidence

_____Showing resistance to change or completing the task

_____Lack of interaction with others

_____Lack of volunteering for new assignments

_____Praising others, but discounting oneself

_____Preferring roles which are supportive rather than leading

_____Completing numerous inconsequential assignments to *"look busy"* while avoiding the more important and riskier tasks

_____Other *(specify)* _____

2. Based on the items you checked off, determine which category or categories you feel are responsible for your team member's deficiency. Check the one or more that apply. *(A deficiency can be related to more than one category.)*

_____Lack Of Knowledge

_____Lack Of Skill

_____Lack Of Motivation

_____Lack Of Confidence

3. If you had difficulty checking off any of the clues in Question # 1, ask yourself whether any of the following additional categories are responsible for the deficiency.

_____Lack Of Technology

_____Lack Of Policies/Procedures

_____Lack Of Vision/Strategic Intent Of The Organization

_____Lack Of Tools

4. Once you understand the reason for the deficiency, you must translate it into a performance improvement requirement statement. Write a requirement statement for your team member.

_____

_____

_____

_____

_____

_____

_____

_____

_____

_____

DETERMINE WAYS TO IMPROVE THE SITUATION

The purpose of coaching becomes clearly evident in this third component of the Coaching Model. Yes, you've observed and monitored performance with respect to an objective, and discovered that your employee has a performance problem. You've also understood the cause of the problem, and have defined the performance improvement requirement. But it's in this part that you decide how to improve the situation and actually begin working on it. And, depending on the competence level of your team members, you will include their input and involve them in the decision-making process.

Monitoring performance and diagnosing performance requirements are critical. However, unless you prescribe a solution, you're no further ahead than when you started. Coaches work on improving performance. In this part of the Coaching Model, you'll determine how to do that. You'll need to select the appropriate form of leadership to address the specific performance improvement requirements of your team members, and you'll put your prescriptions to work.

Matching Solutions To Requirements

Leadership comes in various forms, shapes, and degrees. It's good that it does, for different people respond to various types of leadership in different ways. It's your job as an effective coach to look carefully at each employee's needs and find a solution that will lead to peak performance. Take the time to consider several alternatives before suggesting a change.

Alternatives include *(but are not limited to):*

- ♦ Changing the performance objective

- ♦ Adjusting the performance measure

- ♦ Altering the inputs or information supplied to the employee to achieve the objective

- ♦ Changing the requirements around completion of the objective

- ♦ Altering the process

- ♦ Changing other requirements that impact the employee's time

- ♦ Providing more continuous feedback

- ♦ Introducing new consequences for deficient performance

- ♦ Introducing new learning opportunities

- ♦ Allowing more focused practice time

The solution you choose should eliminate the deficiency and satisfy the performance improvement requirements you have determined. The following table outlines potential solutions for the four deficiency categories: knowledge, skill, motivation, and confidence.

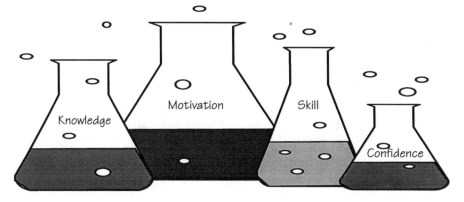

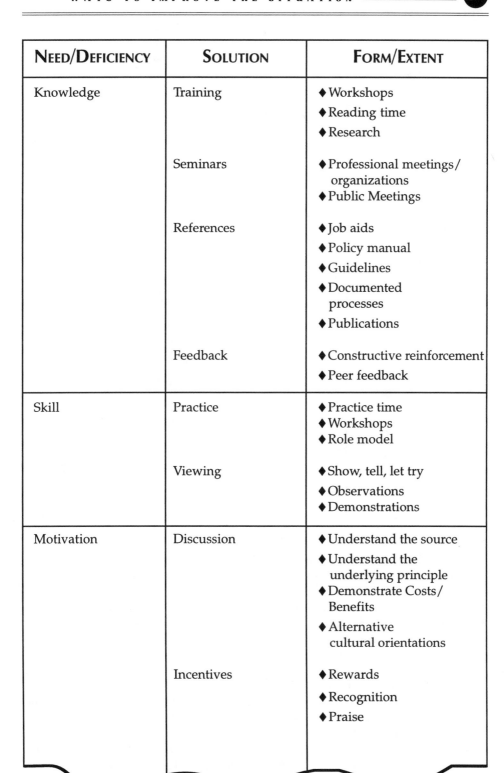

NEED/DEFICIENCY	SOLUTION	FORM/EXTENT
Knowledge	Training	◆ Workshops ◆ Reading time ◆ Research
	Seminars	◆ Professional meetings/ organizations ◆ Public Meetings
	References	◆ Job aids ◆ Policy manual ◆ Guidelines ◆ Documented processes ◆ Publications
	Feedback	◆ Constructive reinforcement ◆ Peer feedback
Skill	Practice	◆ Practice time ◆ Workshops ◆ Role model
	Viewing	◆ Show, tell, let try ◆ Observations ◆ Demonstrations

Motivation	Discussion	◆ Understand the source
		◆ Understand the
		  underlying principle
		◆ Demonstrate Costs/
		  Benefits
		◆ Alternative
		  cultural orientations

	Incentives	◆ Rewards ◆ Recognition ◆ Praise

NEED/DEFICIENCY	SOLUTION	FORM/EXTENT
Motivation	Communication	◆ Assessment tools ◆ Involve in presentations and meetings ◆ Active listening
	Discipline	◆ Stress potential consequences of inappropriate behavior
Confidence	Trust	◆ Words of belief in the person ◆ Self-management ◆ Job enrichments ◆ Star projects ◆ Safe environment ◆ Words of comfort ◆ Learning atmosphere ◆ Okay to ask questions ◆ Failures are opportunities to learn ◆ Role model

Charlene, a restaurant manager...

at an independent dinner house, had been conscientiously monitoring her employees. As a result, she noted that one of her servers, Michael, was having trouble. *"He lags behind the other servers, and some customers have complained,"* Charlene told her assistant manager. In a feedback session, Charlene discussed her observations with Michael and asked for his input. His difficulties weren't related to either attitude or confidence. Michael needed work on his serving skills.

Michael confided to Charlene, *"At the coffee shops where I worked before coming here, we used different computer systems and had different requirements."* Charlene assigned Heather, another server, to mentor and instruct Michael. *"In addition,"* Charlene told Michael, *"I'm going to ask Jimmy, the bartender, to demonstrate to you how to properly open wine bottles. I noticed that it was difficult for you. Jimmy can help."* Michael was both relieved and appreciative. *"Thanks,"* he said. *"Most managers would probably have fired me instead of taking the time to help me succeed."*...

Completing The Performance Progress Sheet

Determining ways to improve the situation is best done in a joint meeting between you and your team member. You need your employee's input for the solution to lead to improved performance.

However, don't assume that the outcome of this task will be obvious. It may require the two of you to work as a team to:

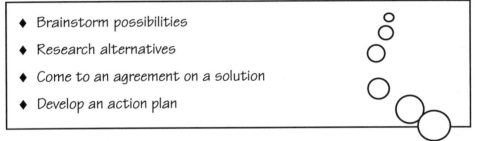

- Brainstorm possibilities
- Research alternatives
- Come to an agreement on a solution
- Develop an action plan

Use the Performance Progress Sheet, and document the agreed-upon solution in the *Action Plan* column. You'll keep the sheet for future reference.

Directing The Employee

Providing direction is an essential skill of leadership. Good coaches know what type of direction and how much direction each team member requires in order to be a peak performer. The amount of direction you provide is contingent upon the needs of the employee and the needs of the organization at the time. In other words, direction is dependent upon the situation. In some cases, you will need to provide a high amount of direction with specific explanation of how to complete the task or assignment, while at other times you can simply delegate the task with minimal levels of direction.

When directing, good coaches focus on:

- Providing structure in terms of goals and roles
- Organizing the workload according to priorities
- Training team members how to complete the task
- Supervising performance and progress toward task accomplishment

PERFORMANCE

Employee	Position/Title	Coach
Misha	Account Representative	Taylor

	BEHAVIOR	DIAGNOSE
DATE	Describe the behavior observed using specific examples and the impacts of the behavior.	Diagnose the cause of the behavior (*i.e., knowledge, skill, motivation, confidence deficiency*). Or, if strength, list the reason.
1/22	Provided incomplete information on the new plan for increasing distribution channels. Missing information prevents the completion of overall department plan.	May lack confidence in selling to new clients. Prefers to call on existing clients. Chose not to complete plan.
1/23	After asking Misha for the report, she was still unable to complete the new plan. This caused further delay of the department plan.	After further evaluation, it is evident that Misha has a lack of confidence for producing the report.
2/10	Sales performance for January was 115% to goal. Revenue and profits were above projections which helps organizational growth.	Increased skills were a result of increased focus on key accounts and capitalizing on special promotions.

PROGRESS SHEET

Department	Period of Performance
National Sales	1/1/XX - 12/31/XX
ACTION PLAN	**RESULTS**
Create an action plan to improve the situation or capitalize on the strength. Decide on specific measurements and evaluation methods along with target date(s).	Revisit the situation and determine if the behavior meets the desired results.
Provide Misha a copy of Kim's plan to show what a good job looks like. Check back tomorrow.	
Have Misha work with Kim on new distribution channel strategy. Kim to share her plan and ideas with Misha first. Misha to revise her plan by 2/22.	
During next National phone meeting on 2/15, have Misha share her experience with the new promotion campaign.	

Sometimes, problems may arise as a result of your employees not understanding what you have asked them to do. Perhaps the specific instructions which you gave were not clear, or this particular team member requires more guidance from you than other members of your team. If, after diagnosing the performance improvement requirement, you determine that the solution is simply the need to clarify your expectations, then restate them clearly and check for understanding. When directing, you must be able to communicate with your employees so that they understand. To do so, you'll need to develop appropriate skills yourself for providing work direction.

Essential steps for providing work direction include:

1. Describe the priority
2. Define the resource limitations
3. Request the employee's input
4. Check for understanding

Take a look at the following descriptions of each step.

❶ Describe the priority

♦ Define the assigned project and its *"linkages"*

♦ Share your expectations and desired results

♦ Discuss measurements and methods

❷ Define the resource limitations

♦ Consider effects on existing priorities

♦ Provide guidelines and offer suggestions

♦ Identify required resources

♦ Determine authority level

♦ Agree to time and resource constraints

♦ Discuss contingency plans

❸ Request the employee's input

♦ Solicit ideas and alternatives

♦ Identify and overcome objections

♦ Mutually agree on a revised plan

❹ Check for understanding

♦ Ask for a restatement of the priority

♦ Establish follow-up dates to monitor progress

♦ Determine feedback process

♦ Be accessible for questions/advice

♦ Explain why

♦ Demonstrate trust in employee's abilities

♦ Gain commitment; reinforce accountability

♦ Provide feedback and recognition for successes

You may find that there are times when no solution or clarification of expectations will work. Sometimes the employee and his job are mismatched. If you discover that your team member doesn't fit his job, then a drastic change is inevitable.

However, the change doesn't necessarily have to be negative. In other words, you don't have to fire every employee who isn't a good match with his or her job. You have many choices for your team member, choices which include:

♦ A new assignment and/or lateral transfer

♦ A special assignment opportunity

♦ A demotion

♦ A promotion

♦ Early retirement

♦ A revised position description

In most organizations a change of this type requires heavy lobbying and paperwork since the change usually will affect another team somewhere in the organization, require a structural change, or require a system change. However, if you desire for your team members to become assets to your organization, you'll find the best place for them.

Janet, the corporate controller...

for a large manufacturing company, was having difficulty with one of her financial analysts, Donna. *"It's not that she's not talented,"* Janet expressed to Derek, her boss. *"She's just unable to deal with our world-wide contacts. Her interpersonal relations with them leaves much to be desired."*

Janet tried to improve Donna's interpersonal skills, but Donna's temperament kept getting in the way. Janet discussed the situation with Donna, and together the two of them decided that it would be best if Donna served the company as a regional financial analyst. *"Your contact with people, especially those of other nationalities, will be more limited,"* Janet explained to her. Donna made the transfer and found herself much better suited to the new position.

Many team members will find these changes to be positive. Promotions can be implemented when employees have simply outgrown their current job responsibilities, and special assignments can be viewed as an *"honorary leave of absence"* from the daily routine. Even a demotion can be positive, if your team member finds the new position to be less stressful. An effective coach looks to make every situation one in which everyone wins.

Tracking The Results

Once you've agreed upon a solution, you'll need to act upon it. Start training your team member, provide rewards, or give increased feedback, if that is what you have decided. Then track the results. Results can be tracked on the Performance Progress Sheet in terms of new behaviors. Remember, you want to document what you actually observe, and measure whether or not the results meet expectations. In some cases, the result will be a tangible measurement such as sales volume or transactions completed.

Tracking the results in this way is preferred since it can become extremely difficult, in some cases, to directly link a new behavior to a specific means of support.

The Performance Progress Sheet is a tool to help you determine how your team member's behavior has changed over the period of performance. You may use this form or create your own. The objective is to provide yourself and your employee with an easy-to-understand tool for monitoring performance over time. This way, when you get to the Evaluating Phase, there won't be any surprises.

If you've provided appropriate support, direction, and feedback, you should be able to observe an improvement in your employee's results on the job. If not, then you will need to support him or her in a different way. If the situation has not improved, first determine the reasons why it didn't. Some reasons include:

♦ The training was designed to teach concepts rather than skills

♦ The individual did not complete the scheduled observation

♦ The mentor assigned did not do his job

♦ The incentive was not in line with the employee's values

At this point, you will need to reassign a different solution and track these results. Again, you may want to use the Performance Progress Sheet for tracking them.

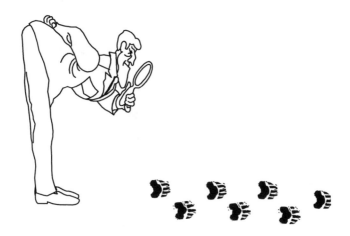

Recognizing Winning Performance

If, after you've begun tracking results, you find that a team member is doing a great job, you need to recognize that performance.

Ever wonder how circus animals are trained to perform such incredible acts? Think about it. How in the world does an animal trainer convince a 300-pound ferocious tiger to jump through a flaming hoop? Very carefully—that's how! And, of course, with plenty of positive reinforcement.

Face it: tigers don't typically stand around the water cooler talking about ways to improve their own performance. Or worse, how to get even with their boss. Furthermore, peak performers of all kinds usually don't start out as winners. Typically, organizations must hire potential winners and develop them over time to become peak performers. In most cases, the use of positive reinforcement is an essential element in achieving desired results.

Positive reinforcement is one of the most powerful tools to motivate people in the work force today. And, not only can it be simple, it doesn't have to cost very much (contrary to popular belief).

An effective coach will create an environment that is motivating to employees while removing barriers and irritants that hold them back. As a coach, ask your team the question:

> "Within our control, what can we regularly provide to our team members to recognize and reward our winning performance?"

There's nothing wrong with being a little creative in selecting ways to positively reinforce your team members' desirable performance. Have some fun with it, too. Whatever you do, make sure that it is appropriate for the behavior, is aligned with your organization's policies, and is perceived to have sufficient value to the employee.

Following are some proven techniques for building team performance. No single *"motivational"* technique will work with all individuals or groups at all times. Since simple and *"common"* events can be more effective than complex and sophisticated interventions, keep an open mind as you consider these ideas. Adapt them to fit your team's needs, interests, and styles.

1. **Tangible Rewards** *(merit increases, special incentives, bonuses, commissions, recognition awards, fringe benefits, variable pay, letters of commendation, paid trips, etc.)*

2. **Status Rewards** *(promotion, improved work area, leadership roles, new title, invitation to critical meetings, private office, etc.)*

3. **Personal Privileges** *(more flexible work hours, time off, more vacation time, special assignments, travel, etc.)*

4. **Job Responsibilities** *(recognition for achievements, praise, job enlargement, job enhancement, increased variety of duties, career advancement, preferential tasks, more resources, replacement assignments, etc.)*

5. **Policies/Procedures** *(relief from repetitive and/or undesirable procedures, opportunity to help create policies/procedures, more access to confidential information, freedom from control/supervision, etc.)*

6. **Work Environment** *(attractive surroundings, less noisy location, more favorable working partners, safer location, stronger sense of job security, etc.)*

7. **Social Activities** *(talking with fellow employees, group lunches, company outings or parties, team-building events, time with senior management, etc.)*

8. **Involvement** *(more participation in decision making; opportunity to influence goals, tasks, and priorities; autonomy; chance to give advice; public recognition; opportunity to train and coach others; opportunity to be a mentor; opportunity to be mentored; involvement in meetings; etc.)*

When it comes to recognizing winning performance, make sure that the behavior is deserving, that the reward is appropriate, and the timing is suitable for the situation. There's nothing worse than rewarding everyone equally when their contributions are unequal. Recognition delivered poorly can be worse than not doing it at all.

As a coach, you'll find that this part of the Coaching Model can be exciting, especially if you see team members reach greater heights of performance. And even if you don't, you know you can continue helping them work toward their specific objectives, or find some way to direct them elsewhere—where they may find success. It's definitely worth the effort you must expend. Keep reading. In the next chapter, you'll learn how to share feedback effectively, a skill every coach needs to master.

CHAPTER FIVE WORKSHEET: DECIDING ON A SOLUTION

1. You identified a team member's deficiency and performance improvement requirement statement in the Chapter Four Worksheet. With that in mind, look at the following table. It outlines potential types of solutions for the four deficiency categories. Circle those that may work for your team member.

NEED/DEFICIENCY	SOLUTION	FORM/EXTENT
Knowledge	Training	◆ Workshops ◆ Reading time ◆ Research
	Seminars	◆ Professional meetings/ organizations ◆ Public Meetings
	References	◆ Job aids ◆ Policy manual ◆ Guidelines ◆ Documented processes ◆ Publications
	Feedback	◆ Constructive reinforcement ◆ Peer feedback
Skill	Practice	◆ Practice time ◆ Workshops ◆ Role model

Need/Deficiency	Solution	Form/Extent
Skill	Viewing	◆ Show, tell, let try ◆ Observations ◆ Demonstrations
Motivation	Discussion	◆ Understand the source ◆ Understand the underlying principle ◆ Demonstrate Costs/Benefits ◆ Alternative cultural orientations
	Incentives	◆ Rewards ◆ Recognition ◆ Praise
	Communication	◆ Assessment tools ◆ Involve in presentations and meetings ◆ Active listening
	Discipline	◆ Stress potential consequences of inappropriate behavior
Confidence	Trust	◆ Words of belief in the person ◆ Self-management ◆ Job enrichments ◆ Star projects ◆ Safe environment ◆ Words of comfort ◆ Learning atmosphere ◆ Okay to ask questions ◆ Failures are opportunities to learn ◆ Role model

SHARE CONSTRUCTIVE FEEDBACK

Providing constructive feedback can be a sensitive and challenging process, but it's one skill every effective coach needs to master. Why? Because it leads to improved performance. Only employees who are aware of their successes and are continually informed of areas that need improvement will make gains. Feedback provides both encouragement and direction.

Giving Feedback Is Part Of Coaching

Throughout the coaching process, you have been proactive in observing job-specific behaviors and providing constructive feedback to your team members. Using the Performance Progress Sheet, you have learned how to document employee behavior as part of each team member's development process. If the behavior did not meet the agreed-upon standards, you identified the type of deficiency—a lack of knowledge, lack of skill, lack of confidence, or a lack of motivation. At times, the deficiencies were linked to the organization's system or environment, not your employee.

Once you identified the deficiency, you learned how to translate the problem into requirements; and, with the appropriate diagnosis, you were able to identify the appropriate solution that best met the situation. Together, you, as the coach, and the team member began to implement a solution that was an all-win solution for the organization.

Now, you will learn how to deliver your message through constructive feedback. Sharing feedback is essential, and it is a major process associated with the next phase of the Performance Management Cycle, known as the Evaluating Phase. However, you shouldn't wait until the annual performance evaluation to unload twelve months' worth of feedback on your team members.

Feedback is not reserved strictly for correcting poor behavior or poor performance. Feedback should also be used as an opportunity to praise your team members by identifying behaviors and results that are noteworthy. Use positive reinforcement whenever you see your employees doing the right thing, or, if they are new at the task, whenever they are doing something approximately right. The process described in this chapter applies equally to team members who are excelling and to team members who need further assistance.

Addressing The Challenges Of Giving Feedback

Improving a situation by offering feedback can be a challenge. Don't complicate matters by making judgments or mandates, which happen to be two of the most common mistakes made. Look at the following examples of *"feedback mistakes"* some coaches make:

Making Judgments   **Imposing Mandates**

Words can build up or destroy. The ones you choose will determine the outcome of your encounter. Words like *"bad attitude," "rude,"* and *"poor team player"* will undermine your objective, which is *"to positively influence behavior and improve situations."*

If you judge an employee as having a *"bad attitude,"* the employee will likely defend himself to the exclusion of all else. This can lead to a verbal tennis match: *"Yes, you do." "No, I don't." "Yes, you do." "No, I don't."* And everyone knows that no one scores in a verbal tennis match.

Describe behaviors

Focus on describing behavior instead. Use specific situations and consequences to support your concerns. You'll diminish defensiveness by sticking to the facts and not veering into a personal attack, and you'll equalize the playing field by acknowledging the other person's position and inviting him to explain further.

For example, instead of blaming an employee who can't seem to master a new piece of equipment, you might say: *"I noticed on two different occasions that you were having difficulty with the new press. Maybe you can help me understand why."* Such a statement is much more conducive to improving performance.

Offer ideas

Mandates are often ineffective because they are one-sided, and they usually lay blame squarely at the feet of the employee to whom you're talking. It's better to address the issue—whether it is a behavior or situation—in all its facets. Usually, there is more than one way to improve a situation.

Offer creative ideas and options, and ask for your team member's input. With effort, undesirable behavior can be creatively eliminated, and desirable behavior can be reinforced. Don't make the mistake of imposing a solution.

Brian was full of new ideas...

Nearly every day, he would stop by his manager's office and share with him his latest concept. *"All right, listen to this,"* he would say, *"I've been thinking about it all night. What if..."* He would then go on to enthusiastically explain his latest and greatest idea. Some of his plans were a bit farfetched. However, when prompted, Brian also had some pretty good ideas about how things should be done around the office. Adam, his manager, knew that Brian's creativity could be put to better use. What Brian needed was some structure attached to his thinking process so that his ideas could become a reality.

Adam began to focus Brian's thinking on his own job-specific objectives. Then, every week during their feedback sessions, Adam would prompt Brian for his thoughts and ideas. *"Brian,"* he would say, *"I've been thinking about your objective for improving our customer data base so that more people will use it. Have you given any more thought about how we might be able to merge our domestic data base with our international data base?"* By focusing Brian on one of his specific objectives, Adam was able to harness Brian's creative energy and guide him toward accomplishing his work-related goals.

Also, by tracking Brian's progress each week, Adam could ensure that Brian's focus remained on the problem at hand. By the third meeting, Brian didn't need to be asked. *"I've got it!"* he said, *"Our data base enables us to use a 5-digit alpha-numeric code to identify the customer. Our current methodology has us combining the two-letter abbreviation for the state with a three-digit numeric number..."* Once Brian got his ideas sorted out, Adam provided just enough direction to get the idea implemented. More importantly, Brian was able to meet his objectives and receive credit for the new idea which was all the reward Brian needed...

In business, coaching is the ongoing process of guiding and developing employees. Performance management is a critical component of being a successful coach. You can become effective at performance management by:

Planning Successful Employee Performance
♦ Incorporate inputs into individual performance plans
♦ Draft or revise performance plans
♦ Finalize the performance plans

Coaching For Peak Employee Performance
♦ Monitor employee performance
♦ Diagnose performance requirements
♦ Determine ways to improve the situation
♦ Share constructive feedback

Evaluating Employee Performance
- Collect and select performance information
- Describe and document behaviors
- Develop and review opportunities for growth
- Conduct and summarize performance evaluation

In the pages that follow, you will learn how to use the Feedback Planner as an effective tool for providing feedback. In addition, you'll be introduced to some skills and strategies you can use during the feedback session itself. The feedback session is a regularly scheduled meeting between you and your team member, in which you will discuss specific objectives.

The Feedback Process

Stage 1: **Describe Current Behaviors**
Describe current behaviors that you want to reinforce *(praise)* or redirect *(reprimand)* to improve a situation.

Stage 2: **Identify Situations**
Identify the specific situation(s) where you observed these behaviors.

Stage 3: **Describe Impacts And Consequences**
Describe the impacts and consequences of the current behaviors on the organization, department, team, or peer group.

Stage 4: **Identify Alternative Behaviors**
Identify alternative behaviors and actions for the coach, the employee, and others to take.

THE FEEDBACK PLANNER	
Name:	Date:
1. DESCRIBE CURRENT BEHAVIORS:	4. IDENTIFY ALTERNATIVE BEHAVIORS:
2. IDENTIFY SITUATIONS:	3. DESCRIBE IMPACTS AND CONSEQUENCES:

The use of the Feedback Planner is an effective way to provide immediate feedback to reinforce or redirect behavior to improve a situation. The purpose of using the Feedback Planner is to create a note-taking worksheet that helps you collect and analyze your thoughts about a situation prior to discussing it with your employee.

The Feedback Planner can help you *"sell"* the need for change to improve a situation. It will assist you in helping others understand the impacts and consequences of their current behaviors, and in addressing areas of needed improvement. It is a tool that can also help your team members realize that they are accountable for their behaviors and subsequent impacts *(good and bad)*, and that they can choose to change their behaviors or the situation to achieve more desirable results.

As you can see, the Feedback Planner contains four boxes. In each box you will list your thoughts of what you might say during the four stages of the feedback process.

Using The Feedback Planner

You can read all the books and watch all the videos you want about flying an airplane or driving a car. However, you will never learn how to fly a plane or drive a car unless you actually sit in the driver's seat and take control. The same holds true for the Feedback Planner. If you want it to work, you must first learn how to use it, and then practice using it before trying it out in the real world. Learn what you can; then take it for a test ride before you try it out on your employees.

> Proper Prior Preparation
> Prevents Pitiful Poor
> Performance

Step 1: Collect your thoughts

Take the blank Feedback Planner and collect all of your initial thoughts about a team member's behavior(s) and a situation by noting them in the appropriate boxes of the Planner. You don't have to fill in the boxes in any particular order. Simply capture ideas as they occur and then revise your notes later.

Step 2: Complete your thoughts

Look for *"holes"* in your Feedback Planner. Have you described the specific behavior(s) in Box 1? Have you identified two to three examples of situations in Box 2? Have you described four to six impacts/consequences in Box 3? Have you identified three to four alternative behaviors and/or actions in Box 4? In this step, you are going for *"quantity"* of information.

Step 3: Revise your thoughts

Use the Feedback Planner strategies listed on the following page to analyze and revise your notes. It's time to address the *"quality"* of information.

Step 4: Discuss your thoughts

Your notes can act as a helpful script to keep you on track during the face-to-face feedback session. They'll help you keep the focus of your discussion to an objective analysis of the situation.

Also, keep your notes as a documentation of your discussion, and give a copy of them to your employee. The notes reveal that you've given the situation careful consideration, and have taken the time to collect and analyze your thoughts. They also show that you have no hidden agendas, and that you're open to other points of view.

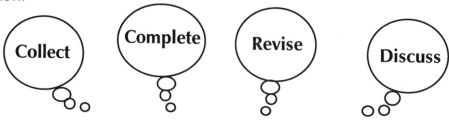

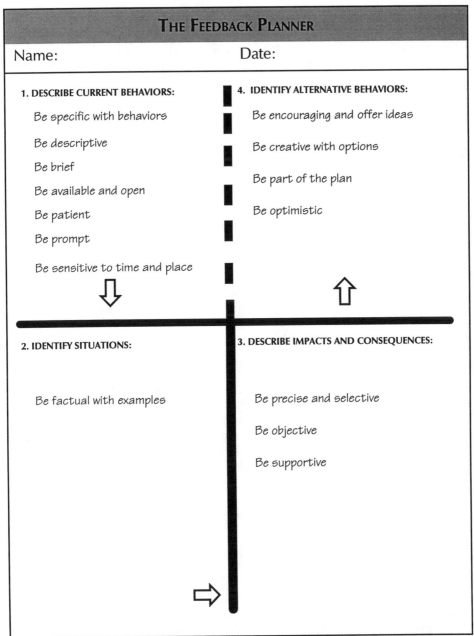

THE FEEDBACK PLANNER

Name: Date:

1. DESCRIBE CURRENT BEHAVIORS:

Be specific with behaviors

Be descriptive

Be brief

Be available and open

Be patient

Be prompt

Be sensitive to time and place

⇩

4. IDENTIFY ALTERNATIVE BEHAVIORS:

Be encouraging and offer ideas

Be creative with options

Be part of the plan

Be optimistic

⇧

2. IDENTIFY SITUATIONS:

Be factual with examples

3. DESCRIBE IMPACTS AND CONSEQUENCES:

Be precise and selective

Be objective

Be supportive

⇨

Additional information and examples regarding the Feedback Planner can be found in the Appendix and in the practical guidebook, *Coaching Through Effective Feedback*, published by Richard Chang Associates, Inc.

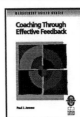

Ed is a sales consultant...

for Spencerville Distributors. Because of the large geographic boundaries of Spencerville's customer base, Ed is on the road most of the time and rarely comes into the office. Ed likes his freedom from the structure and bureaucracy of the office and does whatever it takes to satisfy his customers. Amanda, his manager, has discovered that Ed tends to use the *"My customers come first"* excuse a bit too frequently and often avoids coming to the office for the weekly sales meetings. As a result, Ed has missed several important promotional campaign meetings, resulting in his customers not getting the information they need about the upcoming campaigns.

Amanda realizes that Ed is doing what he thinks is best. However, his unwillingness to attend the sales meetings has actually hurt his customers and his sales are dropping. Recognizing the problem, Amanda calls Ed and schedules a breakfast meeting in Ed's territory. Before the meeting, Amanda prepared by filling out a Feedback Planner.

Amanda began the meeting with some initial discussion about each other's weekend plans. Then Amanda said to Ed, *"You've missed five out of the last nine sales meetings. Each time I ask you why you can't make it, you tell me that you're busy with your customers."* *"That's exactly right,"* replied Ed. *"My customers come first. And besides, if I'm not in the field, my sales will suffer."*

"I appreciate your commitment to your customers," continued Amanda, *"and, I'm sure they rely on your support. However, three weeks ago, Jennifer, the Director of Marketing, outlined the advertising campaign for the new products being released. Because you missed the meeting, most of your customers were out of stock within the first day of the campaign. Had you been to the meeting, you would have been aware of the campaign and could have informed your customers accordingly."* Amanda paused for a moment, before continuing, *"As a result of not informing your customers,"* she said, *"they ran out of stock. Now, their customers are unhappy and your sales are below goal for the third month in a row."*

Amanda went on to explore alternatives for Ed to attend the meetings on a more regular basis. As a result of following the guidelines in the Feedback Planner, Amanda was able to describe the current behavior, use specific examples with actual data, explain the impact and consequences of his behavior, and identify a solution that Ed could agree to. While this news was not fun for Ed to hear, Amanda's use of specific examples to back up her reprimand enabled Ed to agree with the assessment and to realize that his intentions were good but his attitude toward meetings was invalid.

Conducting Feedback Sessions

The best way to deliver feedback is during a face-to-face meeting with the team member to whom you are giving feedback. Effective coaches structure their meetings in order to facilitate communication and make the best use of time. Due to the nature of work in today's organizations, the opportunities to meet face-to-face can be few and far between. However, don't use that as an excuse to conduct such meetings. If used properly, your feedback sessions can achieve higher levels of productivity in less time while maintaining positive and supportive relationships with your team members.

Feedback Sessions:

♦ Provide an opportunity for coaches and individual team members to meet on a regular basis

♦ Help coaches facilitate problem solving sooner than later

♦ Act as checkpoints for the coach and team member to evaluate progress towards the objectives established in the Planning Phase

♦ Strengthen the relationship between the coach and the team member

♦ Should be documented in writing to facilitate the planning of future meetings, act as an agenda during the discussion itself, and assist the coach during the Evaluating Phase

♦ Are best kept to about fifteen to thirty minutes maximum

Meet on a regular basis

Do you ever have too much time left over at the end of the day? If you're like most coaches, the day is too short and the workload is too long. As such, developing your team members to take on more tasks on their own becomes more and more critical. However, it can be somewhat difficult to find the time to meet with all your team members on a regular basis. The solution here is, *"Do it anyway!"*

You depend on your team members, and they depend upon you. Why jeopardize the future of your organization by not taking one or two hours per month to meet with each team member? If you schedule your feedback sessions far enough in advance, commit to keeping the schedule, and honor the time limit agreed upon, you will find the meetings will become *"time savers,"* not *"time wasters."*

How can your feedback sessions actually save you time? Well, problems are like weeds—they keep growing if you leave them alone. When coaches and team members meet on a regular basis, problems tend to surface sooner than later, which enables the coach to help solve the problems. When you meet on a regular basis, problems can be discussed, and together you and your employee can discover a reasonable solution.

Feedback sessions also function as *"progress reports."* In the Planning Phase, you and your team member established performance objectives. During regularly scheduled feedback sessions, you and your team member can determine if the employee is still on course or if he requires an adjustment to his game plan. Objectives are easier to achieve when they are measured and tracked on a regular basis. And, after all, if you can't measure it, you can't manage it. Feedback sessions provide you with the incentive to continue tracking progress and to make any necessary adjustments.

Build relationships

Use the feedback sessions to build relationships. A coach can't help his team members win if he doesn't know what's going on in their lives. This doesn't mean you have to be best friends with your team members. What it does mean is that in order to be responsive to your employees' needs, you must be aware of their personalities and social styles. By knowing your own personality and social style along with that of your team members, you can communicate better and relate better with one another.

Put it in writing

Unless you have a photographic memory, you're better off writing down what happens in your meetings, because more than likely, you will need it later. The need for documentation is critical. Don't get lazy or think that you'll be able to remember all the details, because you won't. Documenting your

feedback sessions will help facilitate the meeting itself by being a discussion guide. Use a document such as the Feedback Planner. It will enable you to stick to your agenda and prevent time-wasting conversation that leads to nowhere.

Documentation of your feedback sessions will also help you prepare for the next meeting. For example, perhaps, as a result of the previous session, your team member had an action item of researching a client's sales history in order to design a strategy for future sales calls. The action plan called for a follow-up conversation to determine if the task had been accomplished. If you don't write it down, you may forget. And, if you forget to ask your team member if she completed the task, you risk one of the two following consequences:

1. If your team member completed the task and you don't ask about it, she may not bring it up because she thinks you didn't feel it was important enough. After all, she remembered to do it, so surely you could remember to ask about it.

—or—

2. If your team member didn't complete the task and you don't ask about it, she may think it wasn't so important after all, and will drop it from her *"to do"* list. Then, if you do finally ask in a later meeting about the status of the task, you will risk sabotaging your team member's trust. She may think you are out to get her.

Finally, the documentation of your sessions will help you compile a formal evaluation of your team members in preparation for the Evaluating Phase of the Performance Management Cycle. No more guesswork. No more forgetting their more significant contributions. No more digging through old notes and files to find the information you need. Clear documentation will end the nightmare of performance evaluation.

Keep it short

Don't drag these meetings on longer than they should be. Fifteen to thirty minutes is all you need if you follow an agenda and stick to the issues that have the greatest impact. If the feedback session takes longer, agree to meet longer or reschedule a follow-up meeting on the spot.

If you find that you can't seem to finish your feedback sessions in less than thirty minutes, a number of reasons may be at fault.

They include:

- ◆ You're not meeting often enough

- ◆ Your team member requires more direction and support than you can personally provide and, therefore, may need a mentor

- ◆ You didn't properly prepare for the meeting

- ◆ Your team member didn't properly prepare for the meeting

- ◆ Your meeting skills need a little work

Keep in mind that feedback sessions don't replace department meetings, team meetings, emergency problem-solving meetings, employee-requested meetings, or any other meeting you may have with your team members. The feedback session is designed to provide you with the opportunity to give feedback to your team members and get an update from them on the status of their objectives. Obviously, there will tend to be some overlap of content from one meeting to another. However, there will also be times when you need to schedule additional feedback sessions during certain projects or with certain team members who require it.

So, use the Feedback Planner, schedule your feedback sessions, and share feedback with each and every one of your team members. They'll appreciate it, you'll save yourself time and trouble down the road, and your organization will reap the rewards of improved performance. It's all part of your job as an effective coach.

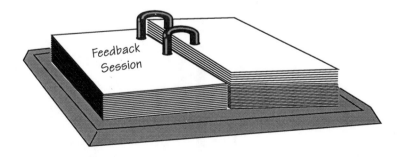

Feedback Session

CHAPTER SIX WORKSHEET: SHARING FEEDBACK WITH YOUR TEAM MEMBERS

1. Think of a recent situation that would require you to give corrective feedback to another person. Describe below the current behavior, and identify the specific situation.

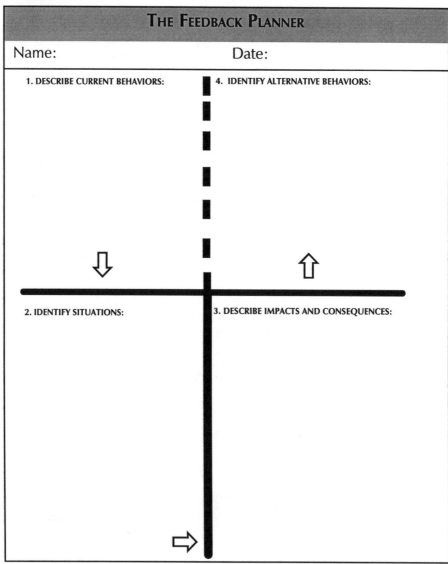

THE FEEDBACK PLANNER

Name: Date:

1. DESCRIBE CURRENT BEHAVIORS:

4. IDENTIFY ALTERNATIVE BEHAVIORS:

2. IDENTIFY SITUATIONS:

3. DESCRIBE IMPACTS AND CONSEQUENCES:

2. Given the previous situation, describe the impact of the behavior, identify alternative behaviors, and come up with an action plan to correct the situation.

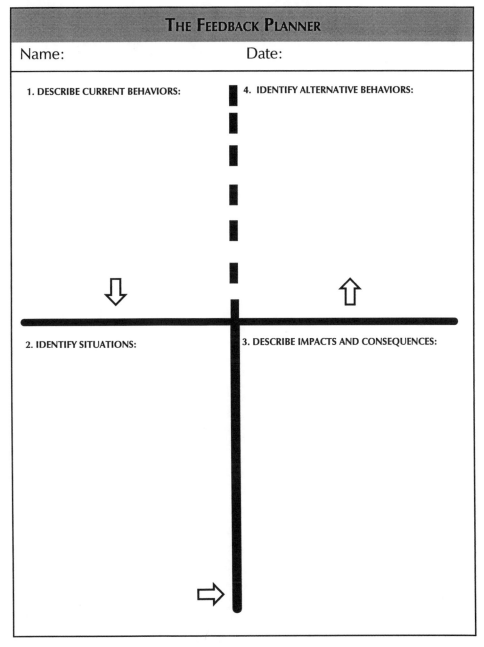

THE FEEDBACK PLANNER

Name: Date:

1. DESCRIBE CURRENT BEHAVIORS: 4. IDENTIFY ALTERNATIVE BEHAVIORS:

2. IDENTIFY SITUATIONS: 3. DESCRIBE IMPACTS AND CONSEQUENCES:

CREATE THE RIGHT ENVIRONMENT

Successful coaches provide support both proactively and reactively. For you to provide immediate support, you must observe behaviors and provide feedback to your team members each and every day. But you must also recognize when extra support is needed, and create the type of atmosphere that encourages acceptance of the direction you provide.

Special Situations That Demand Coaching

There are certain situations that most definitely require extra coaching. Smart managers plan for extra coaching time when they see such events on the horizon. Some of these types of events include:

♦ **The hiring of a new employee**
You probably hired this person because she brings to the job transferable skills, capabilities, and experiences that you believe are required to carry out the responsibilities of the position. However, the environment is new; therefore, extra coaching from you will be needed for orientation, learning organizational norms and practices, and simply learning communication systems (*such as e-mail, voice-mail, etc.*).

♦ **Changes in policies**
When your organization decides to implement a new policy that will directly affect your team members, you'll need to invest extra time and effort in coaching. For example, if upper management has decided that everyone must obtain a badge and display it at all times above the waist for security reasons, this decision (*or policy*) will be accepted by different team members to varying degrees. While some may agree with the new policy and feel it is a necessary practice, others may disagree and find it more of a nuisance.

Don't assume that all employees will accept new policies at face value. In most cases, there will be some individuals who require further explanations, and a rationale for the new requirement. This time required is another form of coaching—*"explaining why."*

♦ **Changes in mission as a result of marketplace demands**

For the past forty years, one organization was in the business of making typewriters. Now this organization must adapt to current market demands and change its mission. The organization is now manufacturing computer keyboards in order to remain competitive. As a result, the coaches are working overtime.

The preceding examples describe a major change that could occur within an organization and that would require coaching. However, coaching is needed when *"any"* change occurs. Other changes come in the form of:

♦ New assignments

♦ Different tools or techniques

♦ Promotions

♦ Demotions

♦ Introduction of new technology

♦ Change in procedures

♦ Employee leave that requires someone to fill in

♦ Upcoming meetings/presentations

♦ Special projects

♦ Relocation

♦ Expansion

♦ Downsizing

Using Tips For Coaching

Knowing when to coach is simply not enough. You must create the type of environment that encourages interaction between managers and team members. Coaching only works in a climate of mutual trust and respect. Your team members must realize that they are not judged by:

♦ Asking what they believe to be *"silly"* questions

♦ Asking too many questions

♦ Asking for help

♦ Asking for direction or support

Several years ago, it was not unusual to find managers in organizations who rated employees low on their performance evaluations if those employees asked questions too frequently of their managers, *(particularly highly-technical research organizations)*. In those days, this type of questioning was viewed as not having the full capability to carry out job duties, and therefore indicated a perceived lack of job skills and knowledge which translated into poor performance.

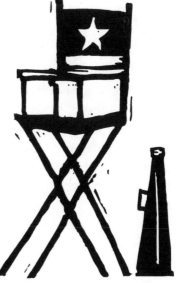

With changes occurring as quickly as they are today, this type of *"rating"* is completely at odds with the need to have open interactions, discussions, and even challenges between team members and their leaders. Only if the atmosphere is one of open communication can a manager truly become a good coach.

Remember, coaching is not the time to judge or evaluate the performance of your team members. Coaching involves taking the time to support, direct, and therefore improve your team members' ability to achieve their performance objectives.

If you want to be an effective coach, take into consideration the following coaching tips:

1. Make the necessary time

Coaching takes time. Although it may be tempting to do something yourself rather than develop someone else or skip giving someone corrective feedback, the time invested will pay off later. Coach today for an empowered staff tomorrow.

2. Be authentic and honest

Coaching only works if you truly want team members to succeed and look for opportunities to develop and stretch their skills. It only works if you give honest feedback and give credit where credit is due. Your team will respect you for these actions, and most likely will strive harder to meet or exceed your expectations.

3. Be accessible

Many managers identify times when they are available or have an *"open door"* policy so that team members can get help whenever they need it. This type of support is important to the people on your team. It also gives you insights into the strengths and weaknesses of your team and allows you to quickly address any deficiencies, thus leading to higher performance.

4. Take into account people's personality and communication styles

Effective team leaders get to know the people on their team and learn what motivates them, what they are concerned with, how they communicate, and how they respond to feedback. All these items come into play when coaching. What works for one individual may not work for another. A coach is sensitive to differences in individuals and adjusts coaching sessions accordingly.

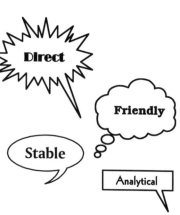

5. Make it okay to fail

A failure means something broke down in the Performance Management Cycle. Perhaps the objective was too much of a stretch for the team member. Perhaps the team leader did not adequately monitor progress or provide constructive feedback in time. Perhaps the needs of the organization changed which required a change in priorities. In any case, everyone can learn from mistakes. A coach can turn failure into a learning experience by working with the team member to analyze what went wrong and what needs improvement. The coach can also help by planning to monitor future opportunities more closely.

DeNece, a divisional vice-president...

in a major sales organization, sat in her office with Scott the day after a disastrous presentation by Scott to 150 field representatives. Frankly, DeNece was surprised. Scott was a very capable manager who was successfully spearheading the development of sales tools for a new product line.

"How do you think your presentation went?" DeNece asked. Scott, nervous about being reprimanded, appreciated DeNece's problem-solving tone. He tentatively offered his perspective, and through direct questioning by DeNece, came to the conclusion that he had focused too heavily on the new innovations and had not prepared the group to accept the change. *"I was too excited about our new product line,"* Scott shared. *"I didn't anticipate the group's resistance and subsequent rebellion to everything I was presenting."*

DeNece and Scott discussed strategies to better introduce the change, and Scott eagerly agreed to address the group again at the next national sales meeting. He knew exactly what he would do next time. DeNece had every confidence that he would succeed.

An effective coach uses every available opportunity to help team members improve and reach their performance targets. It does take time and some training, but the investment is well worth it because it leads to peak performance.

CHAPTER SEVEN WORKSHEET: ANALYZING YOUR COACHING OPPORTUNITIES

1. Check the coaching situations listed below that you have encountered.

    _____ A new employee joined your team

    _____ A new policy or procedure was implemented

    _____ You had to prepare for a special project

    _____ You had the opportunity to build a team

    _____ You had to increase your span of responsibility

    _____ Corporate goals or strategies that affected your team were changed

2. Choose one of the situations that you checked. Describe how you handled the situation.

    _____

    _____

    _____

    _____

    _____

    _____

    _____

    _____

3. Choose one of the situations listed in Question # 1 that is likely to occur sometime soon. How do you plan to handle it?

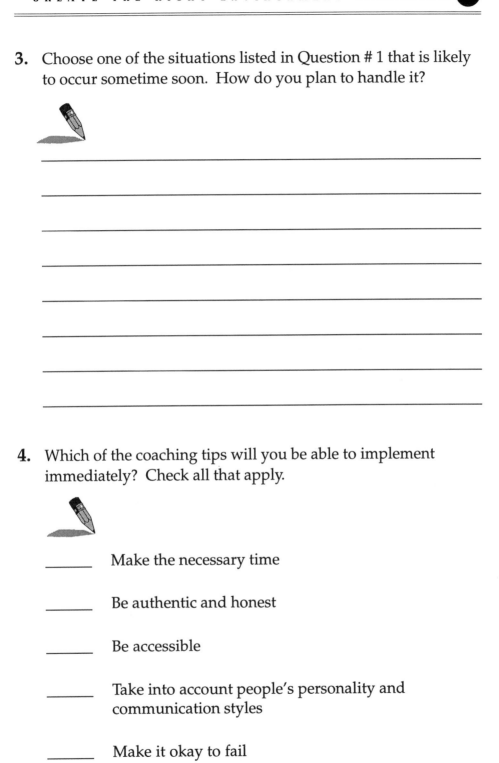

_____

_____

_____

_____

_____

_____

_____

4. Which of the coaching tips will you be able to implement immediately? Check all that apply.

_____   Make the necessary time

_____   Be authentic and honest

_____   Be accessible

_____   Take into account people's personality and communication styles

_____   Make it okay to fail

CHAPTER EIGHT

SUMMARY

It's not all that uncommon to consider coaching as just another form of management. Then again, coaching is also a form of leadership. If you subscribe to the theory that leadership is *doing the right thing* and management is *doing the thing right*, then coaching is *doing the right thing right*. Therefore, the art of coaching involves the strategic influence skills of a leader and the day-to-day operational skills of a manager.

By now, you'll agree that of all the qualities required of a coach, helping your team members achieve their objectives is perhaps the most important. Coaching, as applied to performance management, is the ability to provide the direction and support necessary for your team members to achieve their objectives. As you observe the incremental improvements in their behavior, you'll gain satisfaction in the fact that they are learning. After all, learning is defined as a change in behavior.

Leadership is *doing the right thing*

Management is *doing the thing right*

Coaching is *doing the right thing right*

With the help of performance planning, the role of the coach is simplified, but still not easy. It can be difficult to remember that you are not the *"player."* You can't just step in and do the job yourself. If your team members are ever going to become self-reliant, you must be able to develop their competence *(skills, knowledge, and experience)* in relation to their objectives.

If you follow through with your plans and keep your commitments, improved performance is guaranteed. Coaching is a skill all leaders and managers must do well in order to develop their people. It takes time, effort, practice, and some risk taking. You may be faced with magnificent opportunities brilliantly disguised as impossible situations. Analyze the situations and respond accordingly. Above all, what team members want from their coach is:

1   Honesty

2   Forward Thinking

3   Inspiration

4   Competence

Show people that you are honest in everything you do. Be a change agent—welcome change, and plan for it in a proactive manner. Inspire your team members. Give them the desire to become peak performers by developing them each and every day. And, finally, don't stop learning yourself. Never stop learning and be the best you can be. It's not enough to just learn the tricks of the trade—learn the trade!

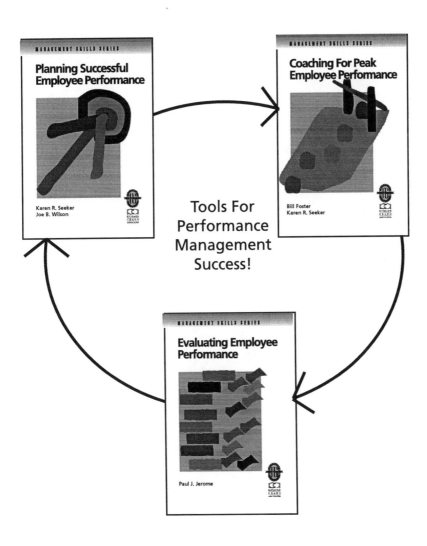

Tools For
Performance
Management
Success!

REPRODUCIBLE FORMS
AND WORKSHEETS

The pages in the Appendix are provided for you to photocopy
and use appropriately.

PERFORMANCE

Employee	Position/Title	Coach

DATE	DESCRIBE BEHAVIOR	DIAGNOSIS
	Describe the behavior observed using specific examples and the impacts of the behavior.	Diagnose the cause of the behavior (*i.e., knowledge, skill, motivation, confidence deficiency*). Or, if strength, list the reason.

PROGRESS SHEET

Department	Period of Performance
ACTION PLAN	**RESULTS**
Create an action plan to improve the situation or capitalize on the strength. Decide on specific measurements and evaluation methods along with target date(s).	Revisit the situation and determine if the behavior meets the desired results.

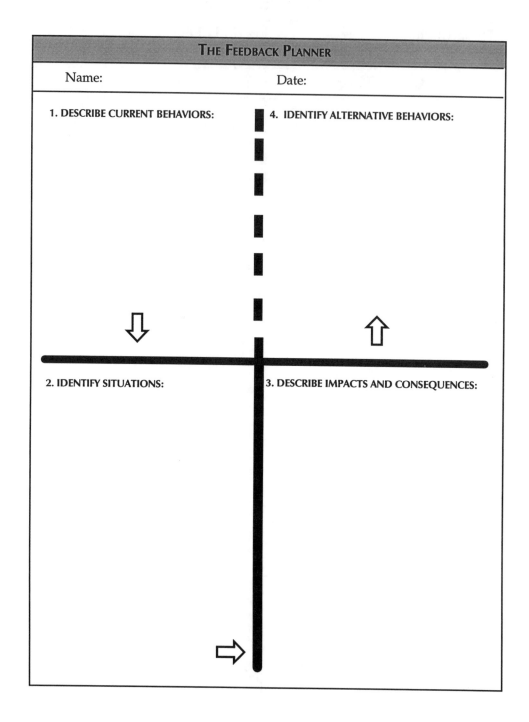

THE FEEDBACK PLANNER

Name: Date:

1. DESCRIBE CURRENT BEHAVIORS: **4. IDENTIFY ALTERNATIVE BEHAVIORS:**

2. IDENTIFY SITUATIONS: **3. DESCRIBE IMPACTS AND CONSEQUENCES:**

PRAISE SAMPLE

THE FEEDBACK PLANNER

Name: Jennifer

Date: 4/3/XX

1. DESCRIBE CURRENT BEHAVIORS:

Recognize Jennifer's recent decisions and actions regarding the client publication, when she . . .

4. IDENTIFY ALTERNATIVE BEHAVIORS:

I will make Jennifer the lead on the *(new client project)* —a project she's very interested in.

I will ask Jennifer if she'd like to take the lead on other projects that she finds interesting and challenging.

I will invite Jennifer to join the design and review committee for a customer service program.

2. IDENTIFY SITUATIONS:

Effectively rebuilt a part of the client publication last Thursday night, personally delivered it to the printer, and waited and brought the finished product back to work on Friday to hand-deliver to the client.

In so doing, Jennifer. . .

3. DESCRIBE IMPACTS AND CONSEQUENCES:

Successfully averted a major crisis with a key client.

Thrilled the client *(and all of us)* with the early delivery of our publication. They said they'd refer new business to us!

Saved our company thousands of dollars *(contractual penalties on a late delivery, and weekend and overtime pay for a bailout effort)*.

Reinforced a strong working relationship with our printer, who avoided a bottleneck that would have occurred with a later reprint.

Acted as a role model for her peers by demonstrating tremendous dedication, initiative, and customer service.

CRITICISM SAMPLE

THE FEEDBACK PLANNER

Name: **Rick**   Date: **2/8/XX**

1. DESCRIBE CURRENT BEHAVIORS:

Rick, I'd like to talk with you about your attendance record for the past two months—specifically, your unscheduled absences due to illness and your late arrivals.

4. IDENTIFY ALTERNATIVE BEHAVIORS:

I'd like to work with you to determine what may be causing you to be late or absent.

Please collect your thoughts and suggestions for immediately improving this situation, and let's regroup tomorrow morning at 8:00 A.M. to build a plan together.

Think about how I or others can help. Maybe we could look at scheduling options? I'm open to just about anything except this behavior continuing.

2. IDENTIFY SITUATIONS:

A. You have called in sick on four nonconsecutive days on (dates and times). That's a total of seven days this year so far (in five months).

B. You have arrived between ten and twenty minutes late on six occasions, specifically on (dates and times).

C. We discussed these concerns twice before on (dates, times and agreements).

3. DESCRIBE IMPACTS AND CONSEQUENCES:

A. A large number of unscheduled absences in a small department causes extra burden for others who are already pressed with a full load. Some work must wait for you to come back, causing delays, overtime, and less work to be processed. You've also exceeded our policy standard of six or less sick days per twelve-month period.

B. Ten to 20 minutes in your job is critical. Our customers expect service when our offices open at 8:00 A.M. When you're not here on time, visitors have to wait for service or leave frustrated.

C. Rick, this is a verbal warning. Further absenteeism and/or late arrivals will result in disciplinary action up to and including termination.

Professional And Personal Development Publications From Richard Chang Associates, Inc.

Designed to support continuous learning, these highly targeted, integrated collections from Richard Chang Associates, Inc. (RCA) help individuals and organizations acquire the knowledge and skills needed to succeed in today's ever-changing workplace. Titles are available through RCA, Jossey-Bass, Inc., fine bookstores, and distributors internationally.

Practical Guidebook Collection

Quality Improvement Series
Continuous Process Improvement
Continuous Improvement Tools, Volume 1
Continuous Improvement Tools, Volume 2
Step-By-Step Problem Solving
Meetings That Work!
Improving Through Benchmarking
Succeeding As A Self-Managed Team
Measuring Organizational Improvement Impact
Process Reengineering In Action
Satisfying Internal Customers First!

Management Skills Series
Interviewing And Selecting High Performers
On-The-Job Orientation And Training
Coaching Through Effective Feedback
Expanding Leadership Impact
Mastering Change Management
Re-Creating Teams During Transitions
Planning Successful Employee Performance
Coaching For Peak Employee Performance
Evaluating Employee Performance

High Performance Team Series
Success Through Teamwork
Building A Dynamic Team
Measuring Team Performance
Team Decision-Making Techniques

High-Impact Training Series
Creating High-Impact Training
Identifying Targeted Training Needs
Mapping A Winning Training Approach
Producing High-Impact Learning Tools
Applying Successful Training Techniques
Measuring The Impact Of Training
Make Your Training Results Last

Workplace Diversity Series
Capitalizing On Workplace Diversity
Successful Staffing In A Diverse Workplace
Team Building For Diverse Work Groups
Communicating In A Diverse Workplace
Tools For Valuing Diversity

Personal Growth And Development Collection

Managing Your Career in a Changing Workplace
Unlocking Your Career Potential
Marketing Yourself and Your Career
Making Career Transitions
Memory Tips For The Forgetful

101 Stupid Things Collection

101 Stupid Things Trainers Do To Sabotage Success
101 Stupid Things Supervisors Do To Sabotage Success
101 Stupid Things Employees Do To Sabotage Success
101 Stupid Things Salespeople Do To Sabotage Success
101 Stupid Things Business Travelers Do To Sabotage Success

ABOUT RICHARD CHANG ASSOCIATES, INC.

Richard Chang Associates, Inc. (RCA) is a multi-disciplinary organizational performance improvement firm. Since 1987, RCA has provided private and public sector clients around the world with the experience, expertise, and resources needed to build capability in such critical areas as process improvement, management development, project management, team performance, performance measurement, and facilitator training. RCA's comprehensive package of services, products, and publications reflect the firm's commitment to practical, innovative approaches and to the achievement of significant, measurable results.

RCA RESOURCES OPTIMIZE ORGANIZATIONAL PERFORMANCE

CONSULTING — Using a broad range of skills, knowledge, and tools, RCA consultants assist clients in developing and implementing a wide range of performance improvement initiatives.

TRAINING — Practical, "real world" training programs are designed with a "take initiative" emphasis. Options include off-the-shelf programs, customized programs, and public and on-site seminars.

CURRICULUM AND MATERIALS DEVELOPMENT — A cost-effective and flexible alternative to internal staffing, RCA can custom-develop and/or customize content to meet both organizational objectives and specific program needs.

VIDEO PRODUCTION — RCA's award-winning, custom video productions provide employees with information in a consistent manner that achieves lasting impact.

PUBLICATIONS — The comprehensive and practical collection of publications from RCA supports organizational training initiatives and self-directed learning.

PACKAGED PROGRAMS — Designed for first-time and experienced trainers alike, these programs offer comprehensive, integrated materials (including selected Practical Guidebooks) that provide a wide range of flexible training options. Choose from:

- Meetings That Work! ToolPAK™
- Step-By-Step Problem Solving ToolKIT™
- Continuous Process Improvement Packaged Training Program
- Continuous Improvement Tools, Volume 1 ToolPAK™
- Continuous Improvement Tools, Volume 2 ToolPAK™
- High Involvement Teamwork™ Packaged Training Program

RICHARD
CHANG
ASSOCIATES

World Class Resources. World Class Results.℠

Richard Chang Associates, Inc.
Corporate Headquarters
15265 Alton Parkway, Suite 300, Irvine, California 92618 USA
(800) 756-8096 • (949) 727-7477 • Fax: (949) 727-7007
E-Mail: info@rca4results.com • www.richardchangassociates.com

U.S. Offices in Irvine and Atlanta • Licensees and Distributors Worldwide